Marketplace
Preaching

Marketplace Preaching

How to Return the Sermon to Where It Belongs

Calvin Miller

Baker Books

A Division of Baker Book House Co
Grand Rapids, Michigan 49516

Published by Baker Books
a division of Baker Book House Company
P.O. Box 6287, Grand Rapids, MI 49516-6287

Third printing, January 1997

Printed in the United States of America

Library of Congress Cataloging-in-Publication Data

Miller, Calvin.
        Marketplace preaching: how to return the sermon to where it belongs / Calvin
Miller.
            p. cm.
        Includes bibliographical references.
        ISBN 0-8010-6320-5
        1. Preaching. I. Title.
BV4211.2.M45 1995
251—dc20   94-32754

Scripture quotations identified KJV are from the King James Version of the Bible.

Scripture quotations identified NIV are from the HOLY BIBLE, NEW INTERNATIONAL
VERSION ®. NIV ®. Copyright © 1973, 1978, 1984 by International Bible Society. Used
by permission of Zondervan Publishing House. All rights reserved.

Scripture quotations identified NASB are from the New American Standard Bible, © The
Lockman Foundation 1960, 1962, 1963, 1968, 1971, 1972, 1973, 1975, 1977.

Contents

110776

Preface

Nurturing the Inner Life

Everything of enduring value begins and ends with Christ. At the outset of this heavily "how to preach" volume, I must raise the issue of "who's to preach." The fundamental credential of preaching is always a question of relationship. What is the preacher's relationship to Christ? Is preaching as a vocation something Christ called the sermonizer to do? Is there any possibility that pulpit drones have gotten it wrong? Even more important than this is the question, What is the 13preacher's right-now relationship to Christ? Are the preacher and Christ walking as one through daily life? Are they together in this very sermon we are now hearing preached? Congregations ought to feel that their leader is a person of God and that the preacher's words come from a relationship that is constantly renewing itself. Congregations want to hear God's Word from one who walks with Christ. Congregations feel deeply that their pastor must know God.

Stephen Covey, in his book 7 *Habits of Highly Effective People,* says that character was once the first issue of all leadership. Not too much is said in most current books on preaching about the pastor's life in Christ. Still, the spiritual life of the pastor far supersedes sermon know-how.

This issue is a book unto itself. Its importance is too vast to be merely a book preface. But the very least that must be said about it falls into two categories. First, the preacher's calling and ongoing life in Christ must be considered, because these two facets harmonize all that is preached with that consistent inward character that typifies the preacher's life. Second, each individual sermon must appear to have been lifted from the altar of pastoral inwardness.

The Preacher's Inner Life

Our inner life in Christ is the defining work of the spiritual disciplines. Therefore, the preacher ought never to pray merely to empower the sermon. The preacher should pray out of spiritual neediness. This yearning after God may sometimes seem to come only out of inferiority or dryness. But to the Father, who supplies all things, it is high desire. God has no wish for us to grovel before him. On the other hand, it is his delight to know that the servant of God is not content to lead the congregation alone.

There are many reasons for nurturing spiritual inwardness. One of the most important is that the success or failure of the sermon will lose some of its power over our mood. Most preachers get their self-worth tightly tied to the sermon's acceptance. I call this the applause syndrome. Preachers have a bit of a problem with hypocrisy in sermon preparation and delivery. If the sermon works, we may appear spiritually coy, giving all the glory to God. If it has *really* worked, we quietly congratulate our egos, taking the credit for it ourselves. When it doesn't work, though, we are usually glad to say, "Well, the Lord just wasn't here today." We imply that if he had been here, the "loser" would have been a real "winner." Winning or losing, the acceptance of our sermons holds an immense psychological power over us. A deeper walk with Christ would free us from this grand elation/deep enslavement polarity. Joseph Seaborn writes:

> I used to go through mini-depressions every Monday. From early in my ministry, I felt compelled to preach the world's greatest sermon every Sunday. And frankly for me I found that was all but impossible. So I hit upon another plan. Now I study hard and work at improving, and when I have done my best, I trust the Spirit of God to make it fruitful beyond my human abilities.[1]

8

But the release from the applause syndrome is no more important than confronting another common sin against our inward spirit. This one is so deep in our subconscious, we are not even aware we are doing it. The answer lies in what Sir James Frazer called the difference between magic and religion. Religion, he said, is the attempt to serve God, and magic is the effect to manipulate God.[2] I know very few sermons, which derive from an inner life, that set out to manipulate God. But I know lots of preachers (how often I have been one!) who believe that God feels very much like they do about the issues of their sermons. This feeling does not come, for the most part, from seeking after God with all our hearts (Jer. 29:13). It comes from the spiritualized presumption that this *must be the will of God because it seems so right to me!*

Reading gives us breadth, study gives us depth, says Jerry Bridges.[3] But the Bible and meditation give us inwardness. I think most every preacher I know works on breadth and depth. But I long to hear those preachers who have pursued the inward dimension. We preachers often preach an inwardness we do not possess. We are sick physicians who spread a kind of contagion by implying we are well enough to heal others. Thomas Watson, the Puritan, wrote:

> Take every word as spoken to ourselves. When the word thunders against sin, think thus: "God means my sins"; when it presseth any duty, "God intends me in this." Many put off Scripture from themselves, as if it only concerned those who lived in the time when it was written; but if you intend to profit by the word, bring it home to yourselves: a medicine will do not good, unless it be applied.[4]

Great sermons are not prepared. At least they do not become great by preparation. They are great because they issue from a preacher whose littleness has dissolved in the immensity of God; from such a life nothing that is little or without consequence can spring forth. Gaining this spiritual immensity can be hard. It may come only as we are brought to the edge of our sanity. A Korean pastor, when asked what has made the churches of Korea such powerful preaching stations in the current time of Eastern revival, replied,

> I think it is because we lived under severe Japanese persecution for so long. We learned to have no hope in ourselves, but only in God. And we learned to pray. We have been a suffering church and, therefore, a praying church. That is what I think explains it.[5]

Great sermons are not born in illustration books but in the needy lives of preachers. Here, where the preacher's inwardness is fashioned by yearning and desperation, is the womb of important preaching.

Lifting the Sermon from the Altar of Pastoral Inwardness

Why must we seek the sermon at our private altar? Why is it so important anyway? Henri Nouwen wrote:

> Our relationships with others easily become needy and greedy, sticky and clinging, dependent and sentimental, exploitative and parasitic, because without the solitude of heart we cannot experience the others as different from ourselves but only as people who can be used for the fulfillment of our own, often hidden, needs.[6]

David Swartz agrees with Nouwen. Swartz further comments on Nouwen and the nature of true worship when he writes:

> Real worship breaks as it lifts. It drains us of pretense and pride, catches us up in the Person of God. It rivets our hopes to His power and majesty and raises deep swells of adoration from our heart that we never knew were there. To worship is to change because we see the living God; no one can behold Him and remain the same. We say we are in His presence all the time. True, but what does it mean to enter the presence of God in worship?
> A retired pastor told me of his closest time in God's presence. Then he added, "But I couldn't stand it for long."[7]

I have admired David Swartz for years. He is a pastor who, in struggling to plant a vibrant congregation, often found himself too needy to seek an easy inwardness that would allow him to preach a cheap grace. To preach the kind of sermons David preaches is to seek the kind of Christ he adores and can never get enough of. Walter Brueggemann has spoken of this spiritual yearning, and we will examine it more deeply later in this book. For the moment, it is important to say that our yearnings define our passions. What we're most hungry for we talk about most ardently to others. There are many clever orators whose preachment is a matter of good communication technique. But there are no great preachers who are this simply defined. Great preachers are great because they lift Sunday's messages, paragraph by paragraph, from the personal altars of their lives.

If there is no personal altar, naturally the sermon must all come from secondary sources. Eugene Peterson, in his glorious paraphrase of Matthew 6:30–33, wrote:

> If God gives such attention to the appearance of wildflowers—most of which are never even seen—don't you think he'll attend to you, take pride in you, do his best for you? What I'm trying to do here is to get you to relax, to not be so preoccupied with *getting*, so you can respond to God's *giving*. People who don't know God and the way he works fuss over these things, but you know both God and how he works. Steep your life in God-reality, God-initiative, God-provisions.[8]

The preacher who does this has found the key to great sermons. Work on building that consistent altar where sermons are gathered from personal adoration. When you become momentarily preoccupied with the compulsion of knowing Christ, you will be ready for the lesser work of sermon-making to which this book is dedicated.

Back to the Marketplace 1

"To stand and drone out a sermon in a kind of articulate snoring to people who are somewhere between awake and asleep must be wretched work," said Charles Haddon Spurgeon.[1] Every preacher faces this unholy fear that wakens ministers at midnight with screaming nightmares of preaching alone in empty churches.

George Bernanos, in *The Diary of a Country Priest,* complained that his congregation was being eaten alive by boredom. "If only God would open my eyes and unseal my ears so that I might behold the face of my parish," he lamented.[2] Solving the problem of such wretched sermons may lie in looking and listening *to* people rather than just talking *at* them. But what can motivate preachers to enter into the conditions of those who listen to them? What can supply the interest and passion that kills boredom? The supply of pulpit power must come from our sense of calling and our worldview. This book, therefore, exists to call preaching back to the marketplace where it had its Acts 2 beginning.

The marketplace made preaching and sermonic interest bedfellows throughout history. This was particularly true at the inception of Christianity. Then every sermon made its preacher a potential martyr. Then church buildings were illegal and sermons had not made friends with Gothic architecture. It was only after Constantine legalized Christianity that worship moved indoors. The illegal sermons of the first two centuries were always preached outside of "churchy" structures. They were often preached out-of-doors! Everything gets more geometric indoors. Walls breed outlines and manuscripts. Homiletics grows somehow with transepts and cubicles. The indoor sermon became housed, and in some cases caged, in worship forms and liturgy. Relevance, for some reason, gets harder to find indoors.

An indoor sermon always runs the risk of becoming more a showpiece and less related than the one preached outside. Outside, in the marketplace, preaching better remembers that Christ commissioned the church to preach the gospel before there were church houses (Matt. 28:18–20).

Why did the church move inside? Why did it abandon the marketplace? Given the politics of acceptance, there were practical reasons. It was noisy outside, and reverence should surround a sermon. Outside everything is threateningly secular; inside it is *safe*. Hence the word *sanctuary!* But what the church did not realize was that it was also threatening inside. The church indoors grows soft. To build a stamina for standing it needs the outside. There it was born to offer itself in a philosophically risky world. In the marketplace, the church is ever reminded of its mission—witnessing. Preaching has as its prime function WITNESS!

The modern Pentecost seems to have failed. The ancient tongues of flame have become only the twinkle lights of spasmodic interest. The church's primary obligation seems almost forgotten. Since 1966 there has been a steady decrease in the size of most "old-line" denominations. This creeping attrition has not shocked Christians back to the primary mandate. The church seems more content to die inside than preach outside. This insidious contentment has produced a view of preaching as a kind of Christian art form. The sermon is often little more than a gallery piece to be critiqued by a congregation of worship reviewers. It has lost its commission. It has come to be treasured, if at all, for its own inherent beauty, style, and soothing togetherness.

Can the sermon escape this piteous end? Only as preachers begin to see the worship hour as a meeting of deep longings. First, there is a longing inside each worshiper to know who he or she is. Each one wants to know where he or she can find meaning and hope. Second, there is a longing in the best of preachers to be used by Christ. Third, there is a deep yearning in the heart of

14

God, who is "not willing that any should perish, but that all should come to repentance" (2 Peter 3:9 KJV). Walter Brueggemann calls the sermon time a meeting of yearnings. "The task of the preacher is to bring to speech that deep yearning. . . . The preaching moment occurs in the midst of this terrible loss and resilient hope. Our speech in the context of loss and hope affirms who we are and what has been promised among us."[3] What has been promised among us is the "reign of Christ, the Kingdom of God!" The sermon must define God's purpose in the world and tell all the parish exactly how everyone fits into that great purpose. The biblical sermon is not looking for critiques or reviews.

If we contrast the sermons of the Reformation or the Great Awakening with those preached today, the difference is usually distinct. History's great preachers existed to call the world to Christ. They saw the sermon *qua* sermon as unimportant. Their sermons were not separate from themselves. Their message existed, as they existed, to call, redeem, and instruct. As a matter of fact, the sermon was indistinguishable from the bearer. The medium was the message. The evangelical church, for all of its success in the seventies and eighties, may be indeed becoming less and less relevant in a fast-paced multicultural society.

A Biblical Call

The prophets of the Old Testament often preached around the temple or in the city center of ancient Jerusalem. One can find in the object-lesson sermons of Jeremiah or Isaiah an album of sociological pictures. These prophets not only preached out-of-doors but made their sermons fit their various object lessons! Jeremiah, for instance, once stumbled through the city under an ox yoke. This image was video ahead of its time. The stumbling icon spoke without words: God would soon put a yoke on the neck of Israel. The impact on his culture would have been less dramatic if Jeremiah had only preached the sermon inside. The same thing may be said of Hosea. He challenged the city by calling his own grievous family life to witness. His miniskirted, go-go wife and ragamuffin children said it all. The judgment and retribution of

15

God fell upon a rebellious culture. Hosea's "domestic homiletic" would hardly have carried the same cultural force had it been preached inside as another "ho-hum" look at Christian Home Week.

The New Testament sermon was launched in a forum format. The forum was the center of Roman civic life. In essence, it was the center of every city. The forum was the place where the town hall spirit of politics and existence flowed for the good (or at least the interest) of all. Oprah, Phil, and Geraldo would later take its place. But once it was the marketplace. There, various "soap-boxers" and "stump preachers" hawked their oratorical wares.

To put the sermon back in the marketplace argues that outside is a better place to preach than inside. Tom Long's *The Witness of Preaching* implies in its very title that preaching is an exposé whose validity is determined only as it is heard.[4]

Preachers seem to come at worship in two distinctly different ways. Baptist and Assembly of God preachers usually talk about what happened in worship. Episcopalians and Presbyterians are more likely to talk about what was said in the sermon. Denominational churches that conclude worship with an "open altar" usually see the sermon as the servant of worship. It is less an exhibit, generally speaking. Evangelical churches are far more likely to see the sermon as a witness to Christ than an altar piece.

"Higher church" persons often object to the infrequent use of the lectionary by evangelicals. Sermons in Baptist and Assembly churches often show an abysmal lack of preparation and study. Nonetheless, these sermons are usually bent more on their mission than their form. Their attempt to bring souls to Christ is so impassioned, there is a disinterest in homiletic form. Mission-centered preaching places a high value on keeping the services relational. Intensity supplants preparation and structure. The components of worship are fiery but eclectic. Structure is perceived as a kind of beast that blockades the easy rapport worship should encourage.

But these denominations are concerned about communicating. They want all that is said to have shopping mall accessibility. "Marketplace" for such churches has relevance. "Marketplace" speaks shopping mall English. Reaching those outside the church demands a highly communicative if less literary style.

This same truth characterizes the megachurches of American evangelicals. Indeed, what has put the "mega" in megachurch is a commitment to a sermon style geared for seekers. Such sermons appear homey and how-to in the worship context that has come to be known as "seeker services." *Praxis* is the whole canon of such marketplace churches. The glory of preaching every Sunday to those outside the church means, of course, that the rhetoric stays so simple that it also appeals to those inside the church.

After his sermon in Nazareth, Jesus was cast out of the synagogue. His only indoor sermon was quickly turned out-of-doors. He seemed to spend most of the rest of his life here on earth preaching in the fields or temple compound. Speaking in this open-air context, Jesus could properly be called a field rabbi. His only entire recorded sermon was the Sermon on the Mount. The sermon on the plain and the temple discourses of Holy Week bear the same kind of witness. "Do you see all these things? . . . I tell you the truth, not one stone here will be left on another; every one will be thrown down," said Christ, preaching his outdoor apocalypse (Matt. 24:2 NIV).

Consider the sermons of Paul. We get the impression again that Paul preached almost entirely in ancient open marketplaces. We know from Acts that Paul preached outdoors on Mars' Hill. While his sermon to Athens was not enthusiastically received, many must have heard him preach it.

The great evangelists who followed in the steps of the Reformation seem also to be marketplace preachers. While Jonathan Edwards, who sparked the first Great Awakening, preached inside, most of the heralds of later awakenings made much of their impact in open-air sermons. The Church of England cold-shouldered Wesley and Whitefield out into the open, crisp air of healthy revivalism.

When the awakenings had spent themselves, the twentieth century saw the birth of mass evangelism. The crusade urgency of Billy Graham and Luis Palau took them to stadiums as the forum for world evangelization. Their video gospel started as an open-air commodity. The remarkable thing about these out-of-doors sermons is that they are transsocial in their reach and impact. Peter Wagner and his church-growth disciples have stated the obvious truism of the current church-growth movement: Churches grow by sociologically homogenous units. After spending nearly twenty-six years in a growing church, I know that Peter Wagner is right. But he is only right if we are speaking of local churches; if we consider the universal church as it experienced its dramatic revivalistic advances, Wagner's thesis is less airtight. Both the awakenings and the modern, mass crusades reach all levels and strata of society.

Buildings themselves do tend to cage societies up in neat little sociological bundles of sameness. Gothic splendor welcomes one kind of communicant; warehouse churches and storefront churches welcome other kinds. Most every sensitive missionary pastor I know laments the Wagner dictum and deplores its truth. Their sense of the mission yearns for the ideal of the marketplace sermon. Preached in small confining architecture, great sermons are pictures longing to break out of their frames. They want to embrace the whole needy transcultural world at once.

When this yearning dies, the sermon is no longer marketplace. It becomes what I shall call here forward the "congregationally-specific" or "local-specific" sermon. This sermon is designed to be heard only by a small, sociologically same, segment of the universal church. This specific congregation ultimately alters the sermon's content and delivery style. It usually shapes it into an art piece critiqued only by those who live within its narrow context of delivery.

Tim Timmons says that the narrow-walled focus of the sermon has been made narrow by three handicaps that the preacher must overcome.[5]

First is the handicap of a world that is listening for all kinds of quick-fix answers. The sermon no longer is the only place people come to find out what the specific answers are to the specific problems. The sermon, in entering this cacophony of ideas, must speak the biblical reply clearly and with passion so that the sermon comes off not just as *an* answer but *the* answer.

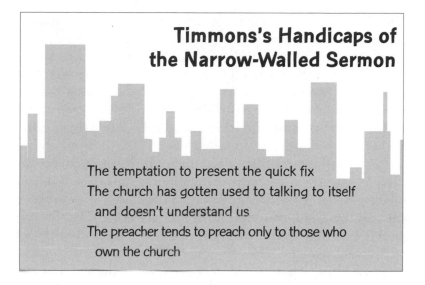

Timmons's Handicaps of the Narrow-Walled Sermon

The temptation to present the quick fix

The church has gotten used to talking to itself and doesn't understand us

The preacher tends to preach only to those who own the church

The second and worse handicap is that the church has gotten used to talking to itself. The church, in building its own radio, TV, and publishing empires, has become so interiorized that it only "reads its own mail" and only "speaks its own interests to the people of Zion." Marketplace preaching is a call to get outside the walls and find out once again what people are talking about and what their interests and needs really are.

The third handicap is that the sermon and largely the worship is prepared to speak and minister to those who "own" the church. Those who come into such self-absorbed worship are not likely to be drawn back. The church must speak to the interests of the marketplace if it is to hold its attention.

In these closing decades of the twentieth century, the sermon has lost nearly all of its transsocial esteem. Only such sermons as those of Martin Luther King Jr. or Desmond Tutu may harken back to the original ideal, and once again, these were often delivered outside the church. Preaching is a polygamist with ugly consorts. Preaching is so married to liturgy, architecture, and popular detente that it spends all its energy in running from wife to wife. It doesn't try to set things right, only to keep from getting things wrong. Sermons are often so dead that dying denominations seem the perfect place to deliver them.

As the various mainline denominations scramble for miracles to keep them alive, maybe they need to go outside once again. Even if they are not physically outside they need to live symbolically outside. Sermons need to learn again the language of the marketplace. So many of the West Coast megachurches have had to meet in public buildings for years before they came up with enough capital to build their own facilities. Their rapid growth may be an indication that marketplace Christianity is hungry once again to be out of its confining architecture. These warehouse temples of extempore worship elbow past liturgies and canned prayers. Could God be signaling that the church's attention is too much centered on buildings? Have these steepled centers of self-congratulation grown to love sermons that have lost interest in meaning? From here on let's refer to the "outside" sermons as those which are market-oriented. Whether or not they are actually preached outside, they exist for "outsiders."

Sermons preached outside have a chance to be heard by those who compose the culture. These churches have shed structured heritage enough that they are able to change. Their verbiage, reasoning, content, and appeal are not for those who "own" the church but for all whom Christ calls the church to "own." Indeed, the very heart of the marketplace sermon is not talking but listening. The marketplace sermon is narratively oriented with a counseling spirit for the hurting urbanites. The outside sermon listens hard because life is hard. The outside sermon is Scripture-saturated, for it knows the Word of God is all that authenticates. Outside sermons teach—but only after they have reasoned and, above all, listened. Outside sermons dialogue; inside sermons tend to pontificate.

The Congregationally-Specific Sermon

The captivity of the modern, inside sermon is lamentable. I do not know of a single clergyperson who does not grieve the slow dying state of old-line denominations. Grief is depressing. It is the antithesis of joy. In the biblical examples of the Sermon on the Mount or the Pentecostal sermon of Peter, the joy is obvious. That same spirit of joy and celebration seems to mark the outdoor crusades of our time. But many shrinking denominational churches seem to be losing members for want of sermonic joy!

Where has this drab sermonizing come from? It seems rooted in *congregationally-specific* sermons. These often arise from a deadly, self-occupying inwardness. There is both a fault and serendipity in lectionary preaching: Its glory is that it systematically covers so much of the Scripture over a few years of time. But somehow it seems to promote structured forms that abandon the freshness of spontaneity. Why? Could it be that spontaneity scares liturgists? In a sense, the lectionary pulpit seems less open to reach for that frightening freedom. This fear can keep the sermon too much an insiders' document.

"Preach to the suffering and you will never lack a congregation," said Joseph Parker. "There is a broken heart in every pew."[6] There is a corollary truth I offer: Preach to the non-church needs and you will never lack a congregation. While those out of church may not have exactly the same needs as those inside the church, their anguish is usually greater. Further, they will have much in common with those inside. Outsiders are interested in learning the power in the name of Jesus. The preacher who meets this kind of outside yearning will likely meet the "yearning Jesus" interests of those inside as well.

But even if "outside" preaching holds no interest to those inside, it is most godly. The church-walled sermon produces a kind of egoism of the redeemed. It is not altruistic. It blocks the very idea of caring widely. Worse than this, inside sermons can become as little as the church's missing *raison d'être*. The church-walled sermon often carries no vision, has no job to do, and thus holds little attraction. Nan Kilkeary says that communication only occurs when we break free of all egoism and enter into others' circumstances.[7] If this is true, only the marketplace sermon is prepared to communicate. The congregationally-specific sermon has generally sold its soul to cloistered interests.

Throughout this book I will use the word *didache* as the function of the sermon that instructs. Conversely, I will use the term

21

kerygma as the force in the sermon that exhorts or motivates. Whether old-line denominational or neo-evangelistic, the inside sermon offers a continual diet of *didache* while *kerygma* alone will supply passion. In no way is this a call to abandon the lectionary text, but it is a call to preach the lectionary text with the larger world in mind. Only then can the preacher fill the prescribed text with a marketplace vitality.

A further encouragement I would call forth is to take some of the sermons outside the church. Leith Anderson, pastor of Woodale Church in Edina, Minnesota, is a marketplace sermonizer. To the glory of both himself and his congregation, he was once given permission to hold their Sunday morning services in a shopping mall. They blessed their community by getting out of their congregationally-specific setting and widening their understanding of what church is really all about. Best of all, they liberated their minds so that even when they worship in their building they still think marketplace!

By contrast, most churches that I visit seem to be shut up in an interiorized worship style. Most of them are preaching messages that "unchurched Harry" (to use Bill Hybels's term) doesn't understand. Therefore, most congregations are preaching to themselves. Their congregationally-specific sermons are safely walled in by the familiar language of Zion. Dwelling in this comfort zone, preaching in many cases has adopted antiquated language forms. Such interiorized churches still depend upon these old, inherited forms. Their soothing sermons enjoy the safety of the province that protects the preacher even as it nibbles at vitality. Their music and worship are also expressed in styles that appeal mostly to their constituency. So many denominational churches have developed their own elegant worship taste, a taste that can be called excellent only within a narrow chasm of appreciation.

The Witness of Preaching

As we have already said, vital preaching has always had as its reason for being the issue of witnessing. Lest we over-celebrate

Tom Long's emphasis on this subject, I need to be honest and say that while Long speaks of the witness of preaching, he is mainly referring to the sermon's witness to salvation and sanctification of those inside the church. The sermons he advocates have at their heart a strong biblical witness to truth. Ian Pitt-Watson of Fuller Seminary sounds a loud and profitable "Amen" to Long when he says that the "What" of our preaching is far more important than the "How" of it.[8] But the idea of witnessing must go beyond the mere telling of truth. Witnessing must ask *why* we are telling this truth. Is it only to form the identity of the church? No, it tells the truth to create the church. Witnessing is to reach as well as teach. It must have a missionary tone to it as well as a doctrinal tone.

Dorothy Sayers (and I first learned this great truth and many others beside from Pitt-Watson) says that the dogma is the drama. It is a powerful drama; it is a drama of content. But it is likely a drama whose glorious excellence is overlooked by those who need it most. For all its excellence, it remains as incomprehensible to the man on the street as Shakespeare would be to Bantu tribesmen. It's time to leave our high-chancel theaters and get the message into street drama. The fastest growing evangelical churches are those that have best remembered this principle. But beware! Such churches may place a high priority on preaching as a way to share their faith with the world but still keep saying these things only to insiders. We "altar call" Baptists always sound like we're preaching outside sermons, but in reality we are only using outside rhetoric that keeps its urgency indoors. This same thing might be said of those with contemporary worship forms. Many churches have moved a long way from customary sermon and worship forms. Still, while utterly nontraditional, they appeal primarily to their own kind of people. This book is not a call for "zoot-suity" sermons and funky homiletical gimmickry. There is as little value in having a noncommunicative contemporary sermon as having a noncommunicative liturgical form!

I would like to examine four shifts in the contemporary culture that accost the "old paradigm" of preaching.

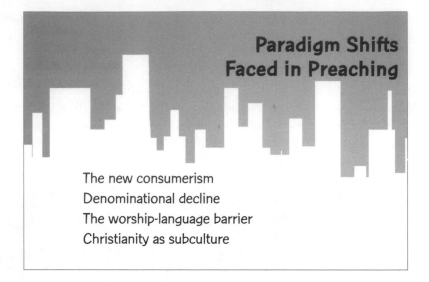

Paradigm Shifts Faced in Preaching

The new consumerism
Denominational decline
The worship-language barrier
Christianity as subculture

Shift Number One: The New Consumerism

George Barna and Bill Hybels have come up with two terms that define the mystique of the new paradigm: George Barna talks about "user-friendly" churches and Bill Hybels talks about "seeker services." Robert Schuller, Bill Hybels, and many other megachurch leaders of our day have encouraged churches to again try to build services that are user friendly. The church is encouraged to be relevant so that the religious consumer will buy into it. Like airline flight attendants, smiling countenances are there to gild the relational appeal of these churches. This new friendliness is to package the gospel attractively. We are thus tempted to trade the demands of Christ for a larger crowd. Only men like Hybels, with the highest commitment to a missionary witness, should be encouraged to downshift from an upfront moral preachment. The sermon's call must *not be lost*!

Marketplace preaching, in the New Testament and other periods of historic awakening, incited men and women to ask, "Sirs, what must I do to be saved?" (Acts 16:30 NIV). When the sermon prompts the question, there must be someone there to answer! The marketplace sermon presupposes altar-centered worship. This does not need to conjure up preaching that trades homiletical excellence for hype-and-neurosis emotionalism. The abuses of the altar call have been many. Nonetheless, the biblical and post-Reformation models of evangelistic sermons often included altars. There still seems to be a linkage between altars and church growth. Altars are traditionally understood as meeting places between God and humanity. Therefore, whether or not there needs to be an actual altar call, the "altar mystique" should characterize great preaching. A sermon that loses its godly summons is at best a current event and at worst a morality monologue.

The business of the sermon and the church has been to call the world to transcendent values. Sermons once pointed to the altar and said, "Come to this place, and let's talk about life everlasting." But in the current secularization of the church, altars have been bypassed in favor of what is being called audience anonymity. Without altars, we talk less and less about eternity and more and more about the here and now!

Once heaven and hell are completely deleted from the sermon, the church will have been culturally domesticated. God must at last surrender his sovereignty to human artifice, for then he will not be found either in the sermon or at the altar.[9] There seems to be a further correlation between the decline of preaching attendance and the church's surrender of the critical issue of transcendence. The modern evangelical church became strong by emphasizing biblical transcendence and growth. To keep sermons from being limited to the here and now, altars must remain places of eternal reckoning.[10] Too often these days, sermons come with little reckoning. Altar calls and public baptism take a back seat to coffee-and-donut communions. A low-demand consumerism and TV cable worship have created the "lite church." Sermons have been supplanted by a gospel-concert mentality that uses Christian weight lifters and glitzy personalities. These gospel stars know enough about entertainment to hold audience attention, but they cannot give their listeners any real biblical reasons to listen.

The call of the sermon seems to be disappearing even as bargain-basement discipleship is on the rise. There are few expensive seats in the growing theater of church growth. The seats must be kept cheap because every attempt to raise the cost of discipleship sends spiritual bargain hunters out shopping for installment-plan faith with a low down payment. The altar demands too much and is abandoned because it has been a detriment to church attendance. Lest we frighten Narcissus away from our assemblies, we rarely bring up the cross. The confused worshiper fails to understand why people get so excited about church while sermons say so little.

Shift Number Two: Denominational Decline

The second shift that accompanies the softness in the contemporary sermon is the decline of denominations. In the year 1966 things changed forever for American denominations. Until 1966, all the American churches were on the grow and some grew rapidly. With that year a decline began to register in nearly every major American denomination. Only Missouri Synod Lutherans and Southern Baptists escaped the early drain on membership. While these two denominations would continue to grow, other denominations were hard hit with membership declines numbering into the millions.

What caused this loss of vitality? Simply put: People will not attend churches they do not perceive as vital or important to their way of life. Long ago, Findley Edge said that people will endure nearly anything in religion except a loss of vitality. Marketplace preaching will reestablish such vitality by learning again of the interests, tastes, and desires of those outside the church and by showing how Christ is adequate to fill them.

Shift Number Three: The Worship-Language Barrier

A third shift that I have long advocated is what I call preaching in the Vulgate. We must remember that the New Testament was not born in colonnaded Greek. Koine Greek is, of course, "street" Greek. The gospel of Christ was written in friendly street language. When Saint Jerome translated the Vulgate Bible in the fourth century, the Bible became once again a Latin Bible but it was also written in street, or Vulgate, Latin. It is no credit to the church that in a few short centuries street Latin would become the language of church liturgy. The very language that once put

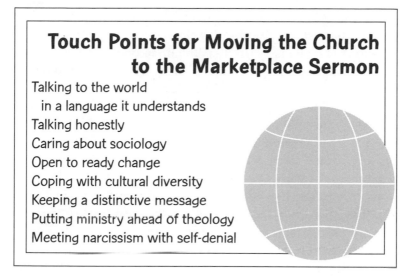

Touch Points for Moving the Church to the Marketplace Sermon

Talking to the world
  in a language it understands
Talking honestly
Caring about sociology
Open to ready change
Coping with cultural diversity
Keeping a distinctive message
Putting ministry ahead of theology
Meeting narcissism with self-denial

religion in the street later removed worship from the *lingua franca* of the people.

The church once again must learn to preach in the Vulgate with marketplace sermons. Preachers must preach conversationally, dropping both Latin liturgy and the stilted clichés of evangelicalism. They must appeal to those outside the church with approachable homiletics.

Shift Number Four: Christianity as Subculture

The fourth shift has seen the church move from a culture to a subculture. This basically suggests that, at one time, church values defined culture. However, the church is no longer central to culture and has become merely a subculture. There are eight touch points that, if achieved, can return the church to her mandate of marketplace preaching.

1. First of all, the church must learn to talk to the world again in a language it understands. The numerical decline of the old-line denominations would say that a mandatory new intelligibility is in fact a psychology of survival.

2. Recent times have witnessed the rise and fall of many Christian television and cable empires. This has precipitated a wide-scale loss of public faith in the church and a loss of respect for

our thin integrity. The church can only regain credibility by learning to talk honestly to the world. Television religion has lost much of its clout. The local church is "in" once again.

3. The marketplace preachers of the third millennium will care more about sociology than did their forebears. The "pro-me" culture of the baby boomers cannot be overlooked. Between the years 1946 and 1964, about seventy-six million babies were born. Those babies now manage corporate and industrial America. They are the nation's thinkers and leaders. Unless the church can quickly learn how this major segment of culture thinks and responds, it can neither appeal to them nor regain its health. We who serve Christ must learn to talk to the "pro-me" culture without sanctioning its narcissism or its permissive morality.

4. The marketplace preaching of tomorrow will understand that it must change its ways or lose the day! The church is about to turn an important millennial corner. Like the entire culture, the church must see that people have a high expectation for life in the twenty-first century. This expectation will come in every area. New areas of social renovation are already in place. More renovation of older social and corporate models will soon begin. Surely this must call Protestants and evangelicals to change the packaging and appeal of the gospel without altering its content. Evangelicals need to undergo what Pope John XXIII called *Aggiornamento* (a redecorating) of many of our old ideas. This search for new forms must be accompanied by genuine and vital discipleship. Preaching must be compassionate enough to care and virile enough to confront an unredeemed society. We must be determined that we will not make preaching a smiling, vacuous response to human need.

5. Marketplace preaching will also have to find ways of coping with cultural diversity. The multicultural division of our country into a melting-pot monolith has now begun to dissolve. What was once called the *Melting-Pot American* now must be called the *Multicultural American*. As any number of sociologists have pointed out, the old melting pot is not melting. These widely independent ethnic and socioeconomic subgroups are demanding more and more individual recognition. These ethnic strata say

openly they have no intention of melting. The explosive competition of these subcultures are blowing our nation apart. It is high time that the church learned to talk the language of the streets in such a way that Christ is not painted as a compassionate Anglo out to reach the other ethnic groups.

Language has become all-important. The pastor now finds a new structure of compassion that demands that we honor everyone's heritage and origin. This goes beyond the mere abandonment of ethnic humor. This ramification ends with clean speech free from every hint of personal judgment.

6. To preach with fervor, marketplace preaching will have to sense that Christianity is special and not just another facet of culture. There has always been a pluralism in America. The difference is that now Christianity is rated by most as the same kind and quality of faith as Islam, New Age, et cetera. Because all these voices clamor with equal intensity, the voice of the church must be heard loud and clear. Its mandate to redeem all of earth's peoples must be called unique. Our missionary evangelism must speak its Jesus-only theology.

7. The church of the future must use preaching to affirm ministry ahead of catechism. Dogmatic theology must soften to pulpit reason. Marketplace preaching will speak in new tones of love and compassion. Reaching new people must be more and more our cause. We can no longer fill our preaching with only high doctrine aimed at those who are unchurched.

8. Finally, the church that challenges the world's narcissism will have to revive those old definitions of missions and evangelism it has too long forsaken. Words like *heathen, lost,* or *Jesus Christ only for salvation*—those ideas, of course, are offensive in a new kind of amalgamated society. Their definitions must remain in force, but we must not use them needlessly to terrorize the lost who no longer think they need them. Everybody in the days ahead will want respect for what they believe, even if their beliefs are spiritually unworthy. This homiletic snare is perhaps the most formidable challenge ever to come upon the church. Universalism is the ravenous new foe of the truly evangelistic church. To call the society "pagan," as C. S. Lewis said, is "too

generous." The word *pagan* assumes at least a belief in a false god. Lewis once said that he would have liked to see the Archbishop of Canterbury lead a bullock to the entrance of Saint Paul's Cathedral and slaughter it in sacrifice to any god. Our day, like his, is only secular—not pagan.

The worst feature of this secularity is that, while it endorses religions, it also endorses equal respect for all viewpoints. The kind of Christian exclusivism that spawned the modern missions movement finds nothing but boos and hisses on television talk shows. To postmodern souls, to call the world to Christ—who alone is salvation—smacks of intolerant exclusivism. So how are we to leap this pit in the missions path?

The urgency of winning the lost lies at the heart of preaching as witness. Unfortunately, the church pastor who declares this too openly will alienate hearers before he or she attracts them. The new pulpit should state the Christian imperative without publicly denigrating any other viewpoint. Since sincerity rather than creed is the primary popular index to being authentic, we must appear sincere. "Be sincere even if you do not mean it" is the new cliché that speaks to our sensitivity. We must appear to be real; and we can most easily make that appearance by actually being real. The church must learn to reach with genuine power in a society that is losing its respect for shabby churchmanship.

Conclusion

The Edsel may have been a great car, but it finally went out of existence and quit being manufactured. It lost out not because it was not a fine automobile but because it was no longer a car that the world wanted. The Edsel was too big and too luxurious in a world wanting smaller, more economical cars. Ford lost the Edsel because it kept asking the wrong questions. Every year they asked themselves how they could make the Edsel better. They just never asked, "Do people want Edsels?" The church itself is always in danger of going out of business if it cannot learn to ask the right questions. The question we should be asking is not how to make our worship services better or our sermons more interesting. The church needs to know what the world *wants* to hear in a sermon, and yet also find a way to give it what it *needs* to hear in a sermon.

This double understanding will mandate many new forms of worship. Sermons that used to end in invitations may not always be able to do that. Whether or not invitations survive, the sense of the altar must. "Come and declare" will have to find a place in the marketplace sermon, however. "Come and declare" are not just words that evangelicals invented. They are the inherent heart of Pentecost. When they are barred from the sermon, the sermon will no longer exist. Still the sermonic forms with which we say, "Come and declare," may radically change. Whatever these new forms are, the church has found the best and most acceptable language to express its faith. This new language, which the church calls forth, will be the building blocks of the marketplace sermon.

The Audio-Video Sermon 2

As the world becomes more secular, it is losing its biblical understanding of who Christ is and what he requires. And the church, by often withdrawing within the cloister of yesterday's worship styles, has lost touch with secular culture and no longer understands what it thinks or believes. Marketplace preaching challenges the church to discover and employ contemporary language, which will enable it to worship and evangelize with power once again. The church must see this calling to contemporize its mission in four different ways.

First, the church must see its primary mission in terms of the Great Commission. Donald Coggin reminds us of the similar meaning of the words *ambassadorship* and *herald*. In 2 Corinthians 5:18–20, Paul says that real ambassadors call enemies to be reconciled! He says again in Ephesians 6:19–20 that he is in chains because he has been declaring the hidden purposes of God. Remember, too, that Jesus takes his text for his ill-received Nazarene sermon from Isaiah 61:1, "The Spirit of the Lord is on me, because he has anointed me to preach good news to the poor . . ." (Luke 4:18 NIV).[1] In light of all this, it is inexcusable that sermons should ever have become so congregationally-specific that they have lost their ambassadorial status. They have talked about Jesus in-house without representing him to those outside the church. The church was born to reach for those outside of Christ. Yet the church has cowered before its secular antagonistic mission field. It has backed away from its redemptionist calling. More and more, its preachment and worship are only for

Contemporizing the Marketplace Mission

1. Make converts

2. Teach a new crowd an old worldview

3. Help the flock to overcome a diminished self-importance

4. Train laity for secular encounter

those who own it. Its local-specific sermons appear to have little interest in making converts. Because of declining membership, many American denominations now appear unable to survive the end of the twentieth century. Even this death threat has not caused them to look with great longing or compassion upon those who do not know Christ. Marketplace preaching must contain a rebuke for this apathetic mind-set.

The second mission of the church is to give its new converts a worldview that is consistent with the teachings of holy Scripture. The marketplace sermon must do more than invite the lost to Christ. Once they come, the church must disciple the newcomers with a New Testament worldview.

How can preaching help inform new converts on covenants? Preaching might use the seasonal emphases of the church calendar to teach these great doctrines. The church at these special seasons will be more open to specific doctrines than on those more ordinary sermon Sundays. For instance, in a sense, Christmas is the best season to teach the incarnation and Easter the empty tomb of Christ. The exaltation of his lordship and sovereignty is a matter for Ascension Sunday. Missions and the Holy Spirit can best be taught on Pentecost.[2] Megachurches may be wary lest their user-friendly mystique is made too specific and offends with heavy doctrine. Still, these churches may find that even the most cautious of the baby boomers are open to learning doctrine if the season is proper. In fact, indoctrination at the right season will be greeted with a festival openness.

The third mission of the church is to help people cope with what it means to be a disciple. In the face of a demanding pluralism, the uniqueness of Christ is diminishing, and so is his agenda for the world. The church and sermon must combat the view that the Christian worldview is only one among many. Every sermon garners force from the worldview and doctrinal beliefs of its preacher.[3] The preacher power that the local-specific sermons sometimes have is almost frightening. While the days of reverencing everything a preacher preaches are over, it remains quite true that the sermon's authority is still in place.

Many church members these days cannot apprehend the call of the sermon because of their own low self-esteem. They want to help and yet they are unable to believe they really have anything important to offer. The sermon must help listeners believe both in Christ and in themselves. This is not just the work of a few specific sermons; it is the work of every sermon. Only when people believe in themselves will they attempt to call the world to Christ.

Fourth, the church must instruct its laity to become proficient in making converts. The church's first emphasis is no longer the perpetuation of its traditions. Tomorrow's emphasis in marketplace preaching must deal with a tougher issue. The real question is: How shall the church exhort a world to come to Christ at all?

The Coming of the Corporate Person

Jeremy Rifkin, in a book called *The Emerging Order,* defined the 1950s as a time when the worldviews of many people began to change. Alvin Toffler, in his book *The Third Wave,* also said that all the world history up to 1750 was involved in the first wave of culture (the agriculture wave). All the world from 1750–1950 he said was the industrial age. Since 1950, we have been experiencing the third wave, a new culture based upon communication. Robert Bellah emphasized some of these same ideas in *Habits of the Heart*. There is wide agreement on the views of these social commentators. The world has indeed changed. It is all-important that the church examine how it must now address this changed world.

The quaint film *It's a Wonderful Life* pictured the inhabitants of an imaginary town called Bedford Falls in the thirties. This nostalgic portrayal that many people enjoy watching is no longer realistic. Such small towns, rural and warm, are gone. Christians will never more enjoy a value system where wonderful old Christmas carols are welcomed by all in a unified world with a unified Christian view. Not Bedford Falls but Hollywood furnishes much of our current value system. Pat Conroy in *Prince of Tides* has now defined where the culture really is. The high incidence of divorce and the decline of the nuclear home defines the context in which the marketplace church must reach.

Back in 1971, Thor Hall wrote an insightful book called *The Future Shape of Preaching*. Even then he could see that the world in the closing years of the twentieth century would be an exodus culture. It would travel away from the old-line institutions that had once dispensed Christianity as a saving hope. Hall suggested that we move on from the term of "post Christian" to the term "post ecclesiastical."[4] This kind of church person would have no interest whatever in traditional church. Current sermon interest must be built around subjects that are freed from the necessity of tipping their hats to denominations and institutions. The power of the sermon now gathers itself totally around a pragmatism that asks, "Why did you bring this up?" and "How is it to be used in my life today?"

The sermon in many ways still maintains a style and perhaps a captivity to the industrial age. For two hundred years the sermon continued to assume that humanity was a maker, a grower, and a pioneer. It still assumes a kind of yesteryear allegiance to small community values. It so often joins small biblical concerns to provincial gatherings of people. When the corporate culture emerged in the 1950s, it was a new phenomenon that the sermon, with its pastoral-nostalgic form, has been slow to address. The phenomenon of corporate, computerized people seemed to threaten evangelicals. So the church began to ignore the New World person who wanted to be greeted with a New World gospel. The hooks and verbiage of sermons that interested the pre-communication-age communicant can no longer be tied to the agricultural, industrial past. Further, it is not immediately clear, in listening to sermons written from this pre-1950 worldview, that there is an understanding of how much the world has changed. The new corporation person is a narcissist. It is harder to challenge the new narcissists with self-sacrifice and commitment. These persons are looking for the self-shelf: self-fulfillment, self-authentication, and self-gratification. In the middle of a confusing culture, marketplace preaching must learn the language everyday people understand and the subjects they are interested in. It is an odd paradox, but only as church members sufficiently believe in themselves will they be able to strip to overload of self from the swarms of narcissists that we need to call to self-abandonment.

The word *colloquial* has often been a dirty word in authoritarian homiletics. Still, people now only listen to those things spoken in their language. Their language must remain somewhat within the confines of a television-generated idiom. Local-specific sermonizing may still intrigue specific congregations with theologically-oriented sermons. But the growing churches have found ways to preach within a newer vernacular! F. Dean Lueking reminds us again that while pulpit authority in our generation should be grounded in the Word of God, it must remain relational.[5] Pulpit language must now be done in "television words." Only in this video vernacular can the sermon shed its yesteryear image.

The corporate narcissist is culturally absorbed with entertainment almost as much as a livelihood. We have become a nation of couch potatoes. We are a culture that "vegges out" after a day's work, crying to the electron tube: "Entertain me!" With the rise of the entertainment culture, we have become image, narrative thinkers. We are the story-soaked! In spite of the fact that we con-

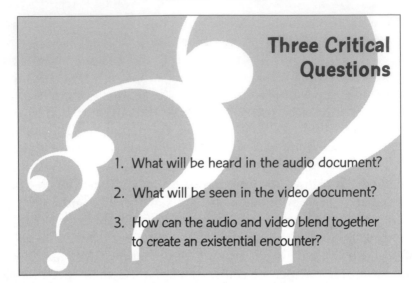

Three Critical Questions

1. What will be heard in the audio document?
2. What will be seen in the video document?
3. How can the audio and video blend together to create an existential encounter?

tinually gluttonize on image, much preaching remains precept-oriented.

Our entertainment orientation has caused all of us to become instant theater critics. Everyone has an opinion on every movie or play introduced into the culture. Sermons, especially in the churches with drama clubs, seem boring. The real question for sermonizers may be this: Can preaching become narrative quickly enough to reach the entertainment age? John Naisbitt says that one of the ten megatrends of the closing years of the twentieth century is the emergence of the arts. We have only to open our eyes to see how true this really is. Our culture in many ways is as decadent as ever. Therefore, preaching will need to call artistically to the culture. This demand upon preachers is immense. They must find artistic ways to satisfy this art hunger while they herald their calls to repentance!

The marketplace sermon will have to take into account three questions. The first question: What will be heard by the worshipers who come within the fellowship? This is what I will be calling the audio document of the sermon. The audio document is that part of the sermon that hearers take in by ear.

The second question must be: What will be imaged in the sermon? In other words, what does the video sermon "look" like?

Preaching is a matter of giving video hope. The video medium paints pictures that the audience is to absorb. These guiding images must be visible, spiritual, and moral encounters. The question of whether television shapes the culture or the culture television is no longer important. That they are now one is no longer debated.[6] The only important question for the church is, Can the church become pictorially video in order to live, or will it remain only audio and die?

The third vital question of sermonic encounter is this: How can the marketplace preacher blend the audio and video sermon to create an existential encounter? Modern people, like those in every age, are souls in search of themselves. The audio sermon, therefore, needs to ask the primary questions of existence: Who am I? Is life worth it? In a day and age in which drugs, alcohol, and suicide have become linked, why do alcoholics, drug addicts, and suicides rarely turn to the church? The church must quickly find the answer to this question. The video sermon must provide images that picture an existential counsel that says "look and live, watch and be healed." The marketplace sermon will answer the ears with saving words and the eyes with healing images.

The Form of the Marketplace Sermon

Preach in the Language of the Street

John P. Newport reminds us that the Scriptures themselves were a combination of "this worldliness" and "otherworldliness."[7] Only as sermons combine the mystical and practical will the combination instruct the church. Whenever we discuss the "streets of gold," the language in which we bring the discussion must come from those streets much nearer at hand. The streets we walk now must provide the language to speak meaningfully of these golden streets where we can't walk yet. The "streets of gold" hold little interest these days for those who must live and die in the gang-war streets at hand. Let the church celebrate its own heritage and traditions if it must. But the church that reaches the unevangelicized world will speak the street language of encounter. The church I pastored for twenty-five years was a church determined to reach people with the gospel of a saving encounter. We determined that, when people walked into our sanctuary and heard us singing, they would hear music that they could relate to. When they heard my preaching, I wanted it to be in familiar words uncluttered by church clichés. I wanted the language of my sermons to be street language! The sermons we ought to preach should be informed by seminary education, but they should be pre-seminary in their style. More of our preaching ought to come from that place where we were when we were called to preach! Peter Marshall, in his famous sermon *The Tap on the Shoulder,* said,

> God calls men to preach. How did preaching arise in the first place? By what right does a man stand before his fellows, Bible in hand, and claim their attention? Not because he is better than they are . . . not because he has attended a theological seminary and studied Hebrew . . . Greek . . . and Theology . . . but primarily because God has whispered to him in the ear and conscripted him for the glorious company of those voices crying in the wilderness of life.[8]

Preachers should remember that they were called out of a human wilderness, and they need to hide their own sermons in that same wilderness language that once appealed to them. The sermon will only speak outside of local-specific congregations if it frees itself from all liturgical bondage. So many churches still sing medieval hymns and preach self-occupied theology. This kind of preaching is always done at the cost of human redemption.

Carry the Affirming Tone of a New Positivism

This idea will doubtless offend some who read this book. But the truth remains that every aspect of modern media is now directed toward the personal. Positivism is the mode of the new consumerism. One has only to look at the success of Robert Schuller or Bill Hybels to understand how utterly important the new positivism is in reaching people outside the church. The church has always thundered a message of repentance. It must

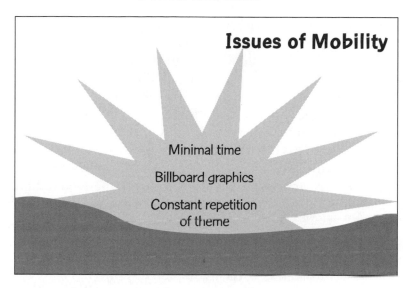

continue to do so. But confrontational, negative condemnations will not reach today's positivists. The marketplace sermon must learn to affirm all persons, saved and unsaved, while we show them the relevancy of repentance.

The Movement of the Sermon Must Be Like Passing Billboards

Sermonic movement must take into account three issues of mobility. First, the sermon must be delivered in minimal time. If there was ever a day and age for a two-hour sermon this is not it! All people now perceive themselves to be busy. Just as movies have gotten shorter and television commercials now flash their fifteen-second messages at us, sermons also must use time economically. Sermonizers must come to see themselves in terms of billboards. As we drive down the interstate at sixty-five miles per hour, billboards get only a blink of our lives to speak to us. The message they carry must be economical—a few words with large, simple images that are both graphic and grabbing.

The second issue of mobility is that minimal time messages must contain maximal information. This kind of confrontation is also a quality of billboards. Billboard images are few and separate; their messages too are of a few, separate words! Yet the billboard words and images instantly combine to make the maximum impact in the shortest time. The marketplace sermon should bear a billboard simplicity—congenial, visual, maximal.

The third issue of mobility lies in the constant repetition of simple messages. From billboard to billboard, we are reminded that the messages we experience are oft-repeated themes. Graphic repetition is the language of a society on the move. The new-millennium sermon will use well-crafted redundancies to champion its ideas. This intentional redundancy will not be offensive. Rather, it will allow hearers to trace the sermon's theme. The rapid-image sermon will teach with creative, planned redundancies while it refuses to relinquish audience attention.

Rehearsing the Dangers

What are the dangers of the audio-video sermon? The first danger is that *the Bible may lose the expository force that furnishes the sermon its real authority.* This must not be allowed to happen. The marketplace sermon should never be divorced from an honest emphasis on biblical exposition. The danger will come in trying to provide all the hooks the preacher needs to snag a secular audience. In holding the attention of the biblically illiterate, preachers will be tempted to move away from the Bible. The megachurches of our day have already received a great deal of criticism for this. It seems that while they know the language of the secular person, they are often not saying anything with scriptural force.

The second danger is that *in trying to find a congenial way to speak to baby boomers, we must not water down the gospel.* Ian Pitt-Watson suggests a sevenfold procedure in sermon preparation that includes a sensitivity to the marketplace and at the same time honors biblical content. His approach reaches backward for content and outward for listeners. Here in a nutshell are his seven steps:

1. Read the text multiple times in Greek and Hebrew if possible.
2. Read the text in alternate translations.

Dangers of the Audio-Video Sermon

Abandonment of expository force

Thinning content just to build rapport

Heritage of "lite" Christianity

3. Read the commentaries (specifically verse by verse: read both generally and contextually).
4. Take a special look at original language word study books of those words drawn from the text.
5. Write a free paraphrase of the verses.
6. Develop in a simple sentence the Scripture theme.
7. Ask yourself all through the development of the sermon from the text, Why this passage? Is there not some passage that does it better?[9]

This seven-step analysis of the text falls rather naturally into two divisions. The first four steps assure that the sermon is teaching the Scriptures. The last three demonstrate that the sermon is being delivered in the vernacular (particularly point five).

The third danger is related to the second: *non-biblical preaching over time will develop only "lite" Christianity.* The world already has little specific understanding of the gospel. Every attempt to lighten up the heaviness of the sermon by pumping it full of airy congeniality will damage the future teaching of the church. Such things as lordship, redemption, and forgiveness are soon lost without Bible-based sermons. We will then grow congregations with a nonsubstantial doctrine that does not help. The

long-range consequence is that the church will cease to pass on its great truths to future generations.

Jude rehearses in verse 3 that such churches at last lose "the faith which was once for all delivered to the saints" (NASB).

Conclusion

I conclude this chapter by offering these three challenges. First, the church needs always to strive for innovative new forms but not new truths. In the succeeding chapters, we will deal with the worship matrix of the sermon. We will look at various sorts of new worship forms—drama, liturgy, oral interpretation, reader's theater, and others. We will examine such components as a call to innovate but not obliterate the church's message.

A second challenge in our emphasis on audio-video preaching will be that we never abridge the truth of the gospel just to gain numbers.

A third challenge is that we must interest our audiences without syncretizing what the Bible teaches with other multicultural values. The history of the church is replete with syncretisms. Syncretism almost always begins by trying to make Christianity more palatable to diverse cultural groups. It is easy to see that the church in the past married various pagan cultures to dilute Christian truths to make disciples. But the result was always the same: usually more was lost than gained. Within our own time, the YMCAs were once formed to weld evangelism to a needy culture. They invited the lost world of that day to come and play basketball and hear about Jesus. A hundred years later, YMCAs function as community centers where one only plays basketball.

Marketplace preaching must not sell its soul to call listeners to the church's congenial messages. The great gymnasium systems of modern megachurches bear an awful similarity to yesterday's YMCAs. In a hundred years such churches who once said, "Come play softball and hear our culture-centered messages," may only say, at last, "come play softball."

If Jeremiah and Jesus risked alienation and public humiliation to deliver their messages, their messages must have mattered a great deal to them. The audio-video sermon is one that inevitably says, "Listen please! Something important is being said! The gospel is still 'the power of God unto salvation'" (see Rom. 1:16). What we do with the sermon is, of course, our own decision to make. If, however, we make Christianity look like a quick-fix course in cheap grace, we will have sold our preachment for pottage.

TelePrompTing the Text 3

In both the worlds of corporate management and the church, contemporary forms of communication are always casual. Throughout evangelicalism exists a strong appeal for the extemporaneous sermon. In the company briefings of the secular world, the corporate mind is also one that prepares tight but hangs loose. Extemporaneous preaching is the mode of the marketplace pulpit. It is always less formal and more friendly than the sermon that is read. But extemporancity must not abandon the issue of authority.

The word *authority* has become the ugly imperative word in an indicative society. Nonetheless, authority supplies passion and interest in every area of communication. If the church can adequately move away from its bias toward old style, theological authority, it may discover a better way to employ authority. Congregationally-specific preaching can still show a good bit of motivational force without appealing to heavy precepts or theological caveats. But the best authority will usually come from two areas: the authority of practical wisdom and the authority of extemporaneity.[1] There is an automatic appreciation these days of the person who has both a good ad-lib style and "content" messages are full of usable wisdom. How different the extemporaneous mode is from the philosophy of those who came before us.

Many older books on preaching still advocate manuscript preaching and formal preparation. But in appealing to the corporate mind, we will need to be lighter on our feet. A well-planned extemporaneous sermon that has done its homework will serve best. The sermon's final form may be a manuscript. In fact, the logic and illustrations of the sermon will flow best only if it is all written out ahead of time. But this document aims at being heard and not read. The manuscript sermon should rarely be read. It should exist to inform the sermon's delivery, but it should not be the sermon.

I am obviously arguing for preparing a manuscript then preaching without it. Preparing the manuscript will allow the preacher to develop skill in sermon crafting. The most mature crafter will use words and phrases in a disciplined way. But when it comes to preaching, a mere outline will give the sermon that deliberate, shoot-from-the-hip, relational force unavailable to the manuscript readers.

What Is Meant by TelePrompTing

To TelePrompt the text is to learn from anchorpersons on the six o'clock news. A TelePrompTer cranks the text of the speech between the lens of the camera and the reporters. They read the text in so casual and direct a way that they appear to be utterly spontaneous in the unfailing roll of words that flow from their lips.

TelePrompTing the sermon text lies in the economical gathering of the sermon manuscript into a sermon brief. This brief should then be committed to memory or transcribed into a few lines of notes that can be inserted into the Bible or the palm of the hand. In those cases where the preacher is delivering several sermons to several different crowds within the same week (as funerals and other engagements demand), written sermon briefs are a must.

If the preacher carries a Bible into the pulpit, these briefs may be recorded onto "tic-tac notes" that can be fixed directly on the page of the Bible. These single-card notes could also be laid on the pulpit. This outline card could also be carried into the pulpit in a coat pocket and referred to as necessary. Since I have preached without a pulpit for the last several years, I have condensed my sermon manuscript to a brief outline affixed directly in my Bible next to my text. Such sermon briefs prompt the fuller essay readily to mind during delivery.

Before we examine how this is to be done, perhaps we need to say that it is really best to be able to preach in at least two modes. In academic settings or formal convocations or lectureships, using a manuscript is the best way to insure saving all the context. Even here, however, it is best to be so familiar with the manuscript that we are in every sense free of it. But in most every other preaching circumstance, extemporaneity welds audience and communicator together. The unnoticeable use of any outline produces a listenable audio document. Now, how do we prepare this audio document?

Preparing the Audio Document: Doing the Text

"Doing the text" is all-important in such preparation. By doing the text, we are talking about looking at the focal passage of Scripture and the sermon logo: we fix in mind the subject of the sermon and then find a text which speaks to that theme. The pastor, of course, should use all of the standard sermon helps (commentaries and various resource books, et cetera) to locate the text that best proclaims the theme of the sermon. The texts that leap at us are not only the simplest, but they drive home their message with authority. Doing the text means granting the text its own communicative force. The text should then be allowed to "hatch" inside the listeners' minds.

The Shape of the Audio Document

For the audio document to have this power, it must be prepared at every step *as an audio document,* not a polished and published religious essay. It must be conceived as something to be spoken even as it is being written! The audio document will come across purely as essay unless the mind serves as the audience during its development. The constant mind-set of the preacher, even during the composition, must be how is this sounding rather than how is this reading.

To help "hear" the sermon, it must be gotten "into the air" somehow—we can only edit it as an oral document if we hear it

Methods of Audio-Editing

Reading it aloud to a friend

Recording it and playing it back

that way. In the process of composition, two approaches get the sermon "into the air" so we can edit it in the audio mode. First and best is the oral reading of the piece to a fellow minister or colleague (spouse perhaps) who can give automatic feedback as to how the piece really sounds.

The second approach is to tape the sermon by reading it from the manuscript and listening to it critically later. This is not the preferred manner of preparing the audio document, since the same weaknesses that cause us to write it without discretion will cause us to listen to it without discretion. Every creator has blind spots that keep him or her from seeing the weaknesses of the created piece. Every sermon composer will both write and listen to the sermon deaf to its deficiencies. If, however, you edit your own sermon using the tape-recorded format, allow a maximum number of days and hours between the recording and the listening process. Time will sharpen your editing with a more critical and objective ear.

Creating Extemporaneity

Creating the extemporaneous feeling in a sermon is not so arduous as it may first appear. Essentially, the longer we hold the sermon in our minds before we preach it, the more it ripens! Sermons not given this maturing time must of necessity be preached "green." The maturing of the sermon demands that it be held within the mind over a period of at least a few days before it is delivered. Richard Baxter, back in the seventeenth century, reminded us that the best preaching is not just thought over for several days before it is preached, but that it is prayed over for several days as well: "Prayer must carry on our work as well as our preaching. For he that does not pray for his people will not preach powerfully to his people. If we do not prevail with God to give them faith and repentance then we are unlikely to prevail with them to believe and to repent." Even sermons "bathed in prayer" must live for a period of time in our minds. Then they can speak with the authority of heaven while they faithfully keep touch with God in the world at hand.[2] Preachers must obviously be preparing weeks ahead of time. They must always be swimming in a pool of upcoming texts. As these texts float in the mind, they will accrete maturing arguments and add issues from current events. Illustrations and anecdotes will also attach themselves in the maturing of the weeks.

Three Tools of Delivery

Sermon preparation can be abetted with three tools, the first being a "sprout book" (a quote and card file and primary everyday source). In this book, life's experiences are recorded so that the events we often pass by become usable. The sprout book must be habitually carried so that we can record these events when they are fresh.

A second tool for shaping the developing sermon is the quote card. Quote cards, unlike the sprout book, will have a formal but authoritative impact. These cards may be paper clipped to the Bible or carried in the pocket. The sources they quote should be properly footnoted and briefly cited before or after the quote is given. Reading directly from the quote card will give a primary-quote authority that summarizing could never do.

Tools of Sermon Delivery

1. The use of the "sprout book"
2. The quote card
3. The primary source

But even more authoritative than using a quote card in the sermon is the carrying of a book, magazine, or news clipping into the pulpit. Reading a great passage directly from a book or other primary source can have maximum impact, but don't overdo it. One of these primary sources per sermon is adequate. To carry in a stack of books at eleven o'clock is usually counterproductive. All of this assumes that the primary source reading will be short and that what is to be read will have been practiced often. Mumbling through a long, intricate passage with the eyes page-locked will connote little force. The value of holding the primary source in the hand is then lost.

Day by day, the sermon components grow into Sunday's art. And the best part is that this maturing sermon preparation attends to the business of life. The best sermons are not prepared in the study. They grow in the front of the mind while the preacher waits for Sunday.

Answering What Communicants Ask

There are two secrets to good logical formation of the extemporaneous sermon outline. First, it is important to prepare yourself to answer what you anticipate people will ask. This is not always

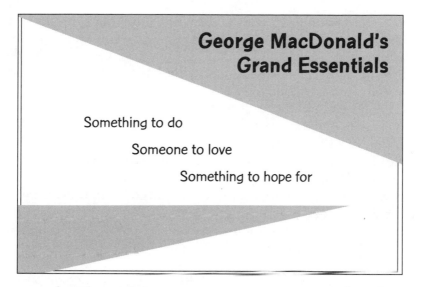

George MacDonald's
Grand Essentials

Something to do

Someone to love

Something to hope for

easy to do. The trick is to prepare your message as though you are the hearer. However, the most damning illusion of sermon writing perhaps lies in the assumption that all people are hungry to know the Bible. Such a hunger, I am afraid, rarely exists outside the church.

This hunger, though, can be created by asking the right questions. These questions will have to do with the meaning of life and people's need to live in and understand their world. Every worthy sermon, therefore, is an existential document. When it ceases to deal with existence, it ceases to be a sermon. A preacher who doesn't know what life's ultimate questions are is no preacher. Like Diogenes, the preacher must thrust his homiletical lantern into the dark fissures of parish lives. This is the heady research of good sermon preparation.

The Primary Questions

What are the primary questions people are asking? These questions have changed somewhat in the past decades. The church's former obsession with the "sweet by and by" has given way to issues of the here and now—sky pie is out. Questions of transcendence are not consuming issues for most baby boomers.

The here-and-now existentialism of the baby boomer is centered in George MacDonald's three *Grand Essentials*. To live meaningfully, said MacDonald, we must have something to do, someone to love, and something to hope for. Out of these issues the questions of sermon validity arise.

Having something to do is the first critical area for which churchgoers seek answers. The idle brain may be the devil's playground, but the idle life is one unconnected to a sense of purpose. The person who seeks answers in this area will be heard to lament, "What have I ever done that matters?" The sermon can answer that question. In terms of the church itself, there is much to be done, and the greatest gift that may follow the sermon is a job—yes, even a church job—for it is the place for idle lives to "plug in," and in the "plug in" is the meaning.

The second issue is not so much a craving to be loved as a need to love someone. Silas Marner, the hermit weaver of Raveloe, was not redeemed in life by finding others who would love him but literally in finding someone he could love. Again, the sermon can answer this question. The sermon that has a heart for ministry can see that those who are lonely need a ministry of their own. A need to minister is basic in most of us. We must have someone to love.

But the greatest question the sermon can answer is the question of hope. Those who heed sermons must always be answered in terms of *Christus Resurrexit*. Christ is the living hope. He is the grand possibility at the center of every sermon. In many ways our day is a bleak one for morality, but the cliché, "the world is going to hell in a handbasket" has never been appropriate. Pannenburg and Moltmann both have reminded us that the church's glory is a theology of hope. Jesus is here and he is coming again. His coming is itself the answer for those who have given up in life. This powerful doctrine must be married to the resurrection. In Christ and his second coming, nothing is hopeless; the sermon must offer all its strategic hope.

Training for Relational Delivery

Ours is a relational day and age. We are not heard very well beyond the borders of our relationships. In spite of this, most

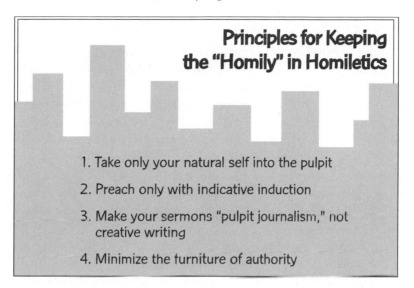

Principles for Keeping the "Homily" in Homiletics

1. Take only your natural self into the pulpit

2. Preach only with indicative induction

3. Make your sermons "pulpit journalism," not creative writing

4. Minimize the furniture of authority

preachers continue to work on content and give very little attention to congregational rapport. Indeed, few preachers really train themselves for relational delivery. So how do we develop that interpersonal oratory that makes sermons live? I believe it is most effectively done by training ourselves to notice how we communicate to people in informal situations. That is, how we get along with people generally. The key is to take all that is natural about our everyday demeanor in our one-on-one relationships, or perhaps in small group relationships, and put those skills to work in the sermon.

As we infuse the sermon with the naturalness of our everyday communication patterns, our delivery will connect.

The Grand Implication of the Word Homily

The grand implication of the word *homily* is this: Conversation and not oratory is the basis of preaching. I would like to offer four guidelines for keeping *conversation* in conversational preaching—for keeping the *homily* in homiletics. Only when dialogue is present in a sermon can preaching live. When these four principles are missing, preaching becomes pedagogy and sermons, lectures.

Principle 1: Take Only Your Natural Self into the Pulpit

Pulpits are haunted by unseen demons that frighten our relational, natural souls into monstrous communicative forms. These demons have little love for the authentic. They prefer pseudo-basso-Sinai-sermon voices and footnoted lectures. They like stiff formality and remote sermon subjects. They pander to churchly ego and congregational pride. Pastor Joey, in this elevated, eleven o'clock light, becomes Dr. Joseph, the lecturer. Being ourselves always seems too little a thing to be in such a lofty place. The organ pipes are tall and so beautifully straight that they beckon us to be like them. We are somehow ashamed to be ourselves in a grand context.

F. B. Meyer, one of the great preachers of England, once asked C. T. Studd, a zealous, newly converted cricket player to give his testimony. Studd gave a none-too-polished but altogether powerful testimony in this austere British pulpit. Following his testimony, Meyer said, "Studd, I am amazed at your power in the pulpit. I would give anything to have such pulpit power." To which Studd replied, "I have nothing you may not have if you are willing to be filled with all the fulness of God." I don't know if the story is real or apocryphal. But if it is real, I wonder if Studd's power may have garnered its strength from a lack of pretense—an utter naturalness—that was not spoiled because he tried to be something august and holy merely because he found himself standing in an august and holy place.

Pulpits strangle all the natural Pastor Jekyll from our lives and change us into a saintly, seminary Dr. Hyde, M.Div., Ph.D. Sometimes, to do homiletics best is not to watch our last videotaped sermon and ask how can we make it better. A better exercise might be to watch an unpolished, nonprofessional home video of ourselves. We might then ask our human and foolish self, How can I get this bumbling, warm, ordinary soul that I am into the pulpit? We must learn to preach a grand sermon without becoming grandiose.

The stuff of the sermon is the full, meaty text of Scripture, packed with things like philosophy, stories, precepts, and statistics. Content is what makes a good sermon. Any number of personality preachers survive on being clever, cute, and personable. But without content, these leave only shallow footprints in the world. For most of us, preaching is having something to say and having to say something. Content grows preachers because they have to dig for it. It grows listeners because they have to grapple with it.

But the danger of content grown too grand is that it makes the speech and speaker grandiose. "A little learning is a dangerous thing," said Alexander Pope. Paul warns us that knowledge puffs us up (1 Cor. 8:1). All preachers can become wise in their own eyes to the point that their naturalness is stolen by a pompous pulpit mystique.

Principle 2: Preach Only with Indicative Induction

Indicative induction creates a pulpit style that avoids dogmatic confrontation. The sermon that contains a lot of "you musts" or "you shoulds" or "God help you if you don'ts" now holds little appeal. We are a generation bred on journalistic style. We have become used to receiving information and then being asked to process it. Heavy imperative preaching was the pulpit tool of another day. "Just give me the facts and stand back while I make up my mind" is the new pulpit policy. Induction leaves listeners free to make their own decisions, and indicative sermons give them the information they need to make those decisions intelligently.

Principle 3: Make Your Sermons "Pulpit Journalism," Not Creative Writing

Walter Brueggemann is right in his Beecher Lectures, *Finally Comes the Poet*. Poetic expression and understanding is sermon ornament and to some degree power. But any poetic preaching mode so heavy with adjectives that it calls attention to its form has lost its mission. I am sold on the Strunk and White admonition for good writing: Write (or preach) with nouns and verbs. Only when the sermon is made solid with nouns and verbs can we go safely back and adorn it with modifiers. Any style where adjectives run wild will lose its natural mode. Once I preached a sermon where I quoted an overlong passage from Shakespeare; upon its sour completion and an empty altar call, I asked a friend how the sermon came off. "It was not too natural," he said. "It was too elite! In fact, I almost came forward to accept Shake-speare as my Savior."

Principle 4: Minimize the Furniture of Authority

This principle is a nice way of saying that you may want to throw out the pulpit. Years ago in a visit to Marble Collegiate Church in New York City, I first heard Norman Vincent Peale preach. I was taken by his utterly relational style. He stood in the middle of a large empty chancel and preached. It was wonderful. He was one of the influences in my decision to throw out my own pulpit.

As a pastor, I had long made it a habit to walk out from behind my desk to counsel those who came to me for help. I never felt comfortable with a desk between myself and crying need. I grew to feel the same way about the pulpit. Once it was removed, it seemed to me the walls of separation came down in worship. We could now talk one-to-one and help each other know Jesus. The sermon, I feel, should be conversation without furniture.

Thinking with a Corporate Mind

There is no automatic way to train ourselves to think with a corporate mind. To preach to the corporate world with any effectiveness means that we must work at understanding the corporate leader.

I recommend three ways to work at such understanding. First, live with your congregation in their world. When I began pastoring in my small Oklahoma parish in the middle 1950s, I found I could lead them into deeper levels of spirituality merely by being with them in their world. I would often go into the fields, get on their John Deere tractors, and ride around with them as they plowed. As I showed interest in their work, they got interested in the God of homiletics.

Years later in a very urban, baby boomer parish, I met with the CEOs of our community for lunch, downtown. I didn't much care for downtown. It was uncomfortably far from suburbia, and it was a long traffic fight to get there. But living in their world taught me their needs and interests and indeed the language of

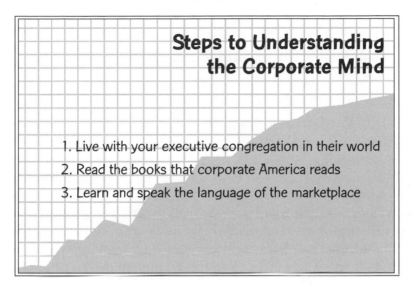

Steps to Understanding the Corporate Mind

1. Live with your executive congregation in their world
2. Read the books that corporate America reads
3. Learn and speak the language of the marketplace

the marketplace. By living in their world, I could preach more relevantly when they came to my world.

Second, all pastors who serve marketplace congregations should read those books that people in the corporations are reading. Promotional, business, and leadership titles are the books that feed corporate America. These books can help us learn to think with a corporate mind.

A third step of learning to think with the corporate mind is to understand that people who work in corporations have a traditional way of relating, a whole glossary of unique terms, and particular ways they use their free time.

In fact, most corporate people define leisure as almost non-communicative. It is increasingly true that once CEO-types are off work, they prefer lounge time. This is the time they debrief their stressed-out minds and deaden their nervous systems. Here at happy hours they shrug off the tight involvement that has consumed their day. When they finally do get home, their thoughts are often still up at the office. This preoccupation keeps them from being the kinds of mothers and dads they should be when they are at home. Only when we immerse ourselves in understanding their business and leisure hours do we have any chance of directing them toward biblical living.

59

Psychological Exposition

Four subjects are of immediate interest to the marketplace communicant.

Security

The first issue is security. There never has been a corporate mind yet that was not interested in this word. In fact, companies are so concerned about it that it often occupies the center of corporate conversation. How does a company stay alive? How does it continue to grow? How does it compete? What does this mean in terms of endurance of the company and those benefits and securities it offers its employees? At the heart of these psychological questions is the fear that the company might fail. Even if it does not, will it allow all employees to remain on the payroll?

Success

If there is ever a word that characterizes the driven dynamic of the marketplace it is *success*! Everybody wants to succeed—nobody wants to fail. To see the importance of this issue one only has to note the utter popularity of positivistic motivators.

We are prone to back away from success as a sermon theme. So much of the popular preaching connected the term with middle-class narcissism. But however the church feels about it, success as a theme dominates the minds in the marketplace. The sermon must at least reckon with this mentality or agree to be judged quaint and out of touch with the times.

Entrepreneurial Mind

The entrepreneurial mind is always incredibly important to those who want to move up in the company structure. At the center of these agendas are suburbia's brightest and best laypeople. The rise of the megachurch in America has seen the rise of the entrepreneurial pastor. However we feel about the success of these business-minded pastors, we must admit they do appeal to the corporate mind-set. They are making their sermons appear effective and relevant to large audiences.

It is important to be creative for the sake of the entrepreneurial

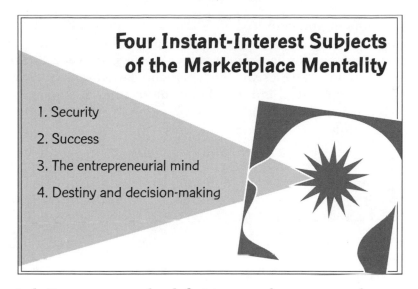

Four Instant-Interest Subjects of the Marketplace Mentality

1. Security
2. Success
3. The entrepreneurial mind
4. Destiny and decision-making

mind. Entrepreneurs by definition are those men and women who apply pressure to the status quo to squeeze from the dry sponge of "what is" things that "should be." Companies appropriately reward employees who come up with significant new ideas. The suburban congregation that cares about infusing old truth with new style will find a ready welcome among those who fashion themselves entrepreneurs.

Destiny and Decision Making

No sermon, I think, that is preached in an evangelical church will want to be preached without some emphasis on the importance of destiny and decision-making. The sermon as persuasion still argues for the right to exist and to call congregations to some kind of decision. This decision must be gently urged. It should be indicatively urged. It must never be bossy or overdirective in any matter. Nonetheless, it must lead naturally to motivate its hearers to do or become something new.

Conclusion

The sermon is not only an audio document but also an extemporaneous audio document. When the text is prepared as a mental document and delivered after thoughtful preparation to the corporate person, it will deal with those psychological values that person understands best. These values are security, success, and the entrepreneurial lifestyle. Such preaching will be welcome because it is thoughtful and sound in its motivation. It emphasizes destiny as it calls for good decision-making in the marketplace congregation.

Indicative and Inductive Truth 4

While this is called the age of information, we must concede that it is also the age of relationships. The marketplace mentality of our age suggests that people attend sermons looking for information, but they come to church in search of relationships. While the church supplies them with friends, this communication age must supply them information in four areas.

Information to Include in a Sermon

Conversion Information

Most of those who also attend Protestant/evangelical churches are aware that churches exist to tell them how to be saved. Most who come are aware that Jesus called himself Savior and that the business of the church is saving souls. While uncomfortable with revivalism, in their minds they still see this as the first work of the church. They expect the sermon and the worship service to provide the information they need to come to God. Since this is a primary expectation, those who come feel that churches which fail to give out this important information are somewhat lacking in worship and preaching.

Growth Information

Whatever the meaning of the word *conversion*, most who hear a sermon will generally feel they are *already* converted. These feel that the church should provide postconversion information that will help them grow in grace. While these words "grow in grace"

Information the Sermon Should Disperse

Conversion information

Growth information

Future-use information

Daily coping information

are churchy, church members want the sermon to communicate the necessary information they need to help them live above all debilitating circumstances.

This secondary information, while not as important as the primary information on how to be saved, should comprise the bulk of the sermons preached. Marketplace Christians will not long attend churches that do not give them practical help.

Pentecostals, Baptists, as well as other evangelistic groups tend to become so interested in evangelizing their communities that they neglect this critical preaching. Since most of the members of the flock are already believers, the sermon should be preached to them. Pulpits that preach only evangelistic sermons are spending 90 percent of their time reaching out to only 5 percent of the people.

Future-Use Information

Another feeling of those who attend church is that pulpit truth ought to be cumulative: They are there to build up a continually growing edifice of biblical understanding. They want to collect a store of spiritual information against some undefined future time of need. The current rage of note taking during sermons would indicate that marketplace baby boomers will likely not remain in attendance at sermons that do not contribute to this equipping for the future.

Daily Coping Information

Speaking to real problems is the big task of the sermon, for most who attend are not interested in saving their eternal souls but in saving the current day. Indeed, to their way of thinking, we save their souls *only* by saving their days.

The most meaningful post-sermon compliments I have ever received were always specific. "This is how your sermon came across to meet this particular need in my life!" The issue of building the "solid information" sermon is the business of this chapter.

Indicative and Inductive Truth

The relationship between inductive and indicative preaching is one of giving the listeners the blocks and letting them build. The word *inductive* implies leadership without coercion. The marketplace mind-set cannot be forced. In this age of Narcissus, the ego is sovereign. For the wise pulpiteer, this means that induction is not merely *a* means of preaching the gospel—it is *the* means.

As induction is in and coercion is out, so indicative is in and imperative is out. "Thus saith the Lord" will always be welcome in the authentic biblical pulpit, but the authority that shouts imperatives must be clearly viewed as coming from Scripture. *Sui generis* is dead and deserves to be. Scriptural authority, however, is quite another matter. It must be allowed to speak its historic correction and hope to the world with all its legitimate authority still intact. Each communicant wants to do his or her own construction of a workable game plan for life. This indicative-inductive synapse is not meant to construct a laissez-faire morality in the church. Parishioners are to include scriptural authority and the demand of God in building their own lifestyles and worldviews. But even at the risk of seeing them come to the wrong conclusion (in the opinion of the preacher), we cannot make these decisions for them. To do this would first violate our strong view of the priesthood of the believer. And second, to violate individual dignity is a kind of authoritarianism all its own.

Staying in Touch with the Basic Ingredients

Staying in touch with the listener's basic needs will determine whether we as preachers are good at our art. Not all of them will deal with problems as we would, but all of them are searching for the same ingredients of meaningful living: ego need, love hunger, self-esteem. We must know and understand the diverse worlds with which they deal.

Indexing the Content of Their Decision

The Bible, accepted by marketplace Christians, must become a users/consumers guide to life. Most people, I think, are spending the "loose" currency of their belief system to purchase all that they can ethically afford. Most all are bargain shoppers: They want to purchase as much meaning with as little spiritual discipline as possible.

The sermon is there serving as an index as to what things count. To these, sin has a practical definition: Sins must be shown to be not only the stuff of bondage but the wrenches in the gearboxes that wreck our moral, consumer system. This is the most effective way the marketplace pulpit can put the price tags on consumer religion.

How does this work? Well, the preacher less and less says "don't sin." He or she leaves that to the discretion (or indiscretion) of the marketplace auditors. He or she says in effect: "Are you tempted to commit adultery? Very well, but here's what adultery costs!" "Do you want a divorce? Then expect to pay this amount." "Cheating on income tax? Involved in office flirtation? Not spending enough time with the children? Very well, but all of these sins have a specific purchase price, and here is what it is."

In marking these price tags, the preacher should make it clear that all are reckoned by a biblical value system. Further, the prices are fixed by Scripture and are nonnegotiable. In this kind of pulpit indexing, the pastor may continue to draw either/or sermonic options while he or she speaks in the indicative and leaves the more imperative "Thus saith the Lords" where they belong.

The Use of Precepts

The Scripture Precept

In this story-oriented culture, we may be prone to neglect the repetition of precepts. But great sermons are ever a mixture of parable and precept. There was a day when our problems repeated these precepts and they became (clichés to be sure) the fabric of our permission and restraints. These precepts will ever be with us: "spare the rod, spoil the child"; "train up a child"; "whatever a man soweth that shall he also reap"; "honor your father and mother"; "don't take the name of the Lord your God in vain"; and so forth.

From the standpoint of selecting a sermon logo from the focal verse, it should be stated as the precept from which the single focus of the sermon is drawn.

The Cultural Epigram

Occasionally, the strong focus of the sermon may be based on a cultural epigram. For instance, I once preached on the McDonald's slogan "You deserve a break today." This cultural epigram served the sermon well because it was tied to a scriptural admonition on Sabbath rest (Heb. 3:14ff). Such cultural epigrams will serve best where they are closely aligned with the focal verse. A warning: Keep them tied to Scripture—they must not be allowed to garner any hermeneutical force apart from Scripture.

Quoting Recognized Authorities

Names themselves are the best source of legitimizing truth. I have a Memorial Day sermon based upon MacArthur's speech from the decks of the battleship *Missouri* on the occasion of Japan's World War II surrender. This sermon illustration has aged a bit since I first used it, but the source of the quote is still recognized and holds general historical esteem. Among evangelicals, C. S. Lewis, for instance, would be a name well recognized and would bear the kind of authority that drives home the intent and context of a sound quote.

Furnishing Illustrations with Authority

Assigning Definition to Illustrations

Illustrations gain a kind of authority for the sermon in two ways. First, they take on specific character. These specifics tend to come in three modes, the first of which is date. Illustrations remain vague and without authority until they are made to face the calendar.

To be specific about specifics, I used to illustrate my own conversion as an indefinite matter of childhood faith. I could make the experience live a bit for those who heard my description of my salvation, but it occurred to me that the event was too vague to really communicate. So I clothed it with definition: I quit saying, "I was a child convert," and began saying, "I committed my life at the age of nine." I further expanded this definition, "I was converted at the age of nine, in August of 1945." From this added bit of information, I further expanded the illustration to say, " . . . not long after the nuclear devastation of two Japanese cities." In this more specific disclosure, I could go on to tell how as a child (because all of my older sisters were married to servicemen) I was a child of Armageddon, watching and grieving with my mother. My mother stood by my sisters who anxiously awaited the return of their husbands from war. Out of this horrible family neurosis and fear, I found what I needed at that crude altar at Tenth and Ash streets in Enid, Oklahoma. There Pentecostals had erected a tent revival . . .

The second specific that makes vague illustrations more concrete is place. In the illustration mentioned above, notice that mentioning not only the city where it happened but the very streets further makes the illustration real.

Names, however, are the most important. Never say, "Let me tell you about a man I once knew." Rather say, "Let me tell you about Bill Jamison." Starting with a real name gives the illustration reality. Adding the names of people, places, and objects serves to make a sermon illustration cry to the hearers, "I am a real story; hear me out!"

Personalizing a Story with Your Involvement

When using a quote in a sermon, relate the story to your own life experience if it is possible. For a long time, I quoted James B. Forrestal's suicide note as an example of the quintessence of despair. When he leapt to his death in 1948, he left behind a note inscribed with some haunting words of the Greek classicist Sophocles:

> When Reason's day
> Sets rayless, joyless, quenched in cold decay
> It is better to die than linger on
> And try to live when the soul's life is gone . . .

It is a haunting and beautiful piece.

I used the verse for years before I finally visited the Forrestal room at Princeton. Seeing the portrait of this Princeton alumnus and famous American statesman, I thought again of his haunting use of Sophocles. Now when I quote Sophocles, I take just a few lines first to tell about my encounter with the Forrestal portrait. Then I call his magnificent despair to view. It personalizes the illustration and gives it force.

I have often used the Leaning Tower of Pisa as an example that we often celebrate things simply because they are crooked. But I always preface this illustration with a specific account of my own encounter with this beautiful but crooked icon of architecture.

All that has been said of storytelling or the use of quotes might also be said of current events. It is especially good to illustrate with current events. But these, too, must have definition. Remember, no one would respect an anchorperson who said, "There was heavy fighting somewhere today." A current event is just that. Events mandate the citation of geography and time, names and meaning. We sermonizers can make any sermonic event live if we supply the best of specifics.

Conclusion

When marketplace people come to the church, they want to spend their attention to purchase information. In such a day as ours, we need to work hard to be sure we are supplying what they seek. Then they may come again and bring their friends to attend something as foolish as preaching—informed, specific, pointed, foolish preaching.

Packaging Preaching: 5
Worship in the Marketplace

Vital preaching can be likened to paratrooper school. No one who is learning how to survive "the jump" needs extra coaching on its importance. In sessions where parachuting is covered, the most mundane lecturer on the subject will have rapt attention.[1] Likewise, the sermon must be so vital that disinterest will carry its own dread penalty. But the vitality of the sermon will gain energy as it moves through a vital worship service. Worship must be so vital that its emotive force warns the sluggish, "Heads up all you who might be prone to sleep through the instruction!" When the parachute instructor rises to the pulpit, it must be even as D. T. Niles once said, "as a dying man to dying men."

In the closing years of the second millennium, one word has loomed ever larger for the church: *worship!* Packaging the sermon in a worship setting conducive to the ever-widening taste of our multicultural world is all-important. Because of the varied worship tastes that abound in America, there are multiplicities of worship styles. Any worshiper looking for a new church can "yellow-page" the way to the exact fit of his or her particular worship preference. When so many tastes abound, is there any objective worship statement to be made? Probably not! Any style of sermon or worship will find some who prefer its individual nuances. Each taste has its own adherents.

The sermon for all tastes, however, must remain the focus in worship. Great worship that trickles through pulpit ineptitude or liturgical deadness is wasted. Worship should say, "Our musicians are ready; our preacher is ready—let's worship!" Worship

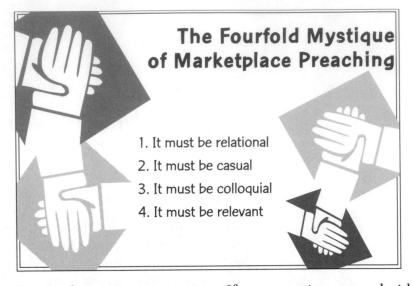

The Fourfold Mystique of Marketplace Preaching

1. It must be relational
2. It must be casual
3. It must be colloquial
4. It must be relevant

enhances these great expectations. If our pastor is possessed with the subject, completely in sympathy with it, he or she will not have to force a message from reluctance. His or her heart is so gorged with what must be said that he or she will only have to open the mouth and the onrush of truth will overwhelm our need with God's supply.[2]

Marketplace preaching will best snuggle into a stylistic worship format that blends with its own preaching style. For the most part, this style of marketplace worship will heed four overwhelming objectives.

First of all, marketplace worship should be *relational*. The predominant psychology of our day is relational. Television abounds with talk shows. Radio offers a totally dialogical format of call-in shows. We live in a "let's talk about it" day and age. The church in touch with this spirit will have a worship style that communicates friendliness and warmth.

Second, this marketplace worship will take on the word *casual*. It is difficult to tell all that this word conveys, but casual worship should be seen in contrast to older, more formal styles. Examining media advertising quickly illustrates that every commercial from cars to fast-food glorifies the casual lifestyle. This same principle packs the churches of Southern California. The style of Sunday dress itself will tell a church where it ranks on the casual-success scale. But the word *casual* refers to more than merely the way worshipers dress. Increasingly casual marketplace churches do not have choirs. If they do, often they are not robed. The pastor who preaches may or may not wear a suit and tie.

The third adjective for marketplace worship is *colloquial*. Rhetoric was once the stuff of great sermons. Now the entire tone of worship must be conversation. In fact, the word *homily* means "chat." While the oratory of great preachers like Beecher or Brooks or McLaren might have bypassed the simplest meaning of the word, the basic definition of homiletics perfectly fits the marketplace sermon of our day. "Chat" is the four-letter word that must become the definition of colloquial worship.

The final word is *relevant*. Great worship has always honored the term. But today the hard driving urchins of Wall Street will not listen long to anything that doesn't apply to them. Further, marketplace persons must catch hold of sermon relevance within the first few moments they attend it. If they begin to worship and it seems to have no *immediate* meaning, they will not listen at all. Sitting in a long service where candles burn and a robed choir sings a near-Latin anthem condemns current worship as an ineffective matrix for the voice of God. Relevance means, as David H. C. Read once said, that most contemporary listeners are not nearly so interested in where Cain got his wife as they want to know whether or not they should stop sleeping with a girlfriend.[3] Marketplace relevance never forgets the moral milieu of the now.

All four of these words—*relational, casual, colloquial,* and *relevant*—define what I call "Vulgate worship." By this term I simply mean worship must exist *for* and be understood *by* the person on the street.

The megachurches of our day have exploded in size because they have majored on worship that has its genesis in the Vulgate culture. The number-one worship rule of these successful marketplace megachurches has been in every case: *Start with people where they are, not where you wish they were!* Vulgate worship is the only plausible answer for the modern corporate mind, with its urgent right-now need and its hypercritical concepts.

With this philosophical definition in mind, let us turn to music and other worship support forms. Remember, some of those things that we most often consider to be a need of the church are not really needs at all. Even those items that George Gallup has discovered and certified by poll do not necessarily track. A. J. Conyers says that while most Americans believe in heaven, according to a Gallup poll, they do not act out their "faith" in crises.[4] Only those areas where the church reaches people where they are can be labeled "relevant."

Music

Congregational Tastes

Musical taste in every congregation is always varied. Still, the wise worship leader must stay in touch with those tastes. To test this diversity, sit down at a radio and listen to the many styles and formats of modern programming. They are multifold: easy listening, hard rock, soul, lite rock, lite country, total country, classical, jazz, and so on. But listening to the radio for even a moment reveals that the broad center of culture has a household acquaintance with middle-of-the-road tastes. The more a congregation seeks to reach out to those outside the church, the more it will have to honor their taste; the less it cares about outreach, the more it will seek to humor the musical taste of those inside the church. It will, in seeing its own constituency as all-important, become congregationally-specific rather than marketplace in its preachment as well. Most times musical tastes reflect only the stilted preferences of those conditioned by traditional training. They are for the most part singing to themselves (and generally preaching to themselves as well) without much genuine concern for the taste of those outside their fellowship.

Tempo

Musical tempo, like taste, knows no fixed rules. But to appeal to the marketplace mentality the cadence must move. While some hymns and anthems may call for a quiet and serene speed, too much slow music leaves the tone funereal. A brisk tempo achieves

Congregational Music in Marketplace Worship

It must fit congregational tastes

It must have a brisk tempo, at least from time to time

It must be "hummable"

It must link the local church to the church universal

at least two things. First, it will set the listening pace for the entire service and particularly for the sermon. Worship must set a brisk listening pace, and the sermon must continue that pace. Søren Kierkegaard reminds all preachers from generation to generation that truth is never "nimble on its feet." Fred Craddock, in *Overhearing the Gospel,* also reminds us that even the greatest of truths can be rather pedestrian.[5] A slow tempo sins by setting a lethargic listening pace that says "listen slow." Congregations thronged with business persons will generally want both the sermon and the worship style to say, "We promise not to waste your time with a creeping encounter."

Brisk music further connotes the idea that some impending impact is likely to occur. A good music style says we are rushing toward a great moment of truth and personal change. The music shows that we are excited about all that this change will mean in our lives.

"Hummability"

A. A. Milne's Winnie-the-Pooh was entranced with the inward quality of what he called *hums.* Hummable music is residual and leaves the communicants singing their way out of Sunday and into the week. Such music has connected! Indeed, all marketplace worship should contain a lilting dynamic that warmly motivates us to act, live, and decide out there beyond the benediction.

In essence, the hummability of worship is the sack in which the hermeneutic (scriptural application) and the homiletic (sermon delivery) get bagged for later use. Most people bring hummability home from a Broadway play or a country-western concert. They won't attend musical events that don't leave them wanting to sing. The churches that have a popularly attended service must do similar packaging. Music becomes the mortar of the church, and when it is warm and relational (and ultimately hummable), people feel close. People sing themselves into a unit in church, much as they cheer themselves into a unit at an athletic event. Do marketplace churches ever honor music in its more classic expression? Of course. The church must make some room for the great music of the church. The church, as Pope John XXIII long ago reminded us, must be for every generation both *Mater et Magistra* (Mother and Teacher). The church should teach worship and teach people an increasingly widening taste. Still, church musicians who are bent on instantly moving whole congregations to classic liturgy may be forced to do it unaccompanied.

Advent and Eastertide, as well as Pentecost or any great season of worship, is a natural time to use the traditional music of the church. Such times will say that the grandest themes of incarnational theology cannot be illustrated with mere hand-clapping or praise ditties. A further key to congregational acceptance will be not just in doing the great music of the church but in doing it well. Many times high church music does not sell because it is so poorly done. In such cases, what lay critics are reacting to is not unrelational music but squalid performance. We need to remember at this and other moments C. S. Lewis's warning that "holy shoddy" is still "shoddy."

Linking the Local Church to the Church Universal

We should never make a god of contemporaneity. Every church that ministers to the marketplace mentality needs to make an effort to remind its urbanized clientele that the church has been around a few centuries and survived other idiosyncratic tastes. It is a sin to let marketplace taste in worship and music deny the church its long-standing history of great music. Still, as we said before, to reach urbanites we must ever begin where they are and not where we wish they were.

Support Forms

Special Music

The marketplace church exists in a culture nourished on entertainment. Neil Postman, in his *Amusing Ourselves to Death,* says that the metaphor city of the West is Las Vegas. This glitzy entertainment mecca defines all that most Americans call good music and good times. Therefore, "special music," whether taped or with live accompaniment, may better serve and relate if it is set free of organ thunder. The soloists and ensembles of the marketplace church, though, may appear too "Las Vegas" for many traditionalists. However, synthesizers and combo arrangements are the common currency of musical taste, so it is time we learned from many of the successful megachurches that have traded formal choirs for combos.

Drama

Drama is being rediscovered in marketplace worship. Drama, like special music, serves best when it prefaces or concludes the sermon. Having tried drama in the church in every context, I must say that I like it best when it augments and enhances the sermon, rather than when it tries to replace it.

Drama may take two forms. The first (and my preference) is the drama that is done symbolically to act out or comment directly on a passage of Scripture. I use the word *symbolically* because symbolic drama intersects the Bible passage or truth and illustrates or defines it.

This kind of drama may be acted out by tableau figures in pantomime while a narrator does the reading. This is particularly effective in those churches where there may not be enough competent actors to pull off a full-scale professional interpretation. Or actors may be used in dramatic dialogues. The key is to make the symbolic interpretation as professional as possible.

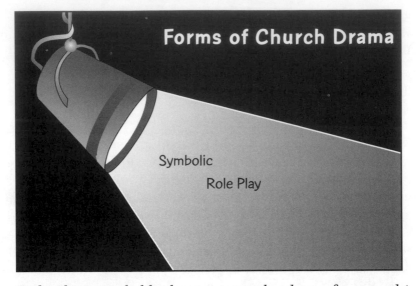

Forms of Church Drama

Symbolic

Role Play

Role play is probably the most popular drama form used in churches. This kind of drama does not interpret the Scripture text. It does not symbolize it. It merely parallels it. This kind of dramatic presentation lacks the visual sticking power of the symbolic approach. Further, it is less effective in demonstrating Scripture. The symbolic drama will go much further in helping people learn and remember the sermon Scripture. Whatever we do to contrive worship, it must be a real Sunday-to-Sunday occupation of our lives. John Killenger has called preachers to be the entrepreneurs of worship. The title may lead us into extravagances of trial and error, in which the errors will be humiliating or comic or melodramatic. But it is probably much better to err on the side of attempting the new than playing it safe with business as usual.[6]

Other Worship Forms

There are many other worship forms that might be used. I will discuss four possibilities here.

Sign language groups. Deaf church members will inevitably desire to be used in worship, as well they should be. A deaf choir can perform marvelous interpretations and worship themes. Sometimes these themes can be set to musical interpretations (these, of course, have to be coached and choreographed by someone who can hear). Sometimes they perform in total silence, but always the experience is beautiful and worshipful.

Pageant. Easter, Christmas, Thanksgiving, and the Fourth of July are occasions where marketplace churches may gear their talent and drive toward community encounter. The various worship forces—drama, music, orchestra, video—may all join in a marvelous community effort to involve the community. (Columbus Day and the Fourth of July now have less appeal in highly ethnic groups where multiculturalism can be confrontive.)

Mime and dance. Both mime and dance can also be used effectively in meaningful worship. The more professional these groups are, the higher degree of their impact. It is especially important that interpretive dances use taste in dress and movement. This artistic worship form is a powerful force in the church, but it still must pay for its right to serve with good taste. There is something about dancing that lifts despair with lightness. It is impossible, I think, to dance and despair or to dance and doubt. There is such immense power in the dance that I wonder why all churches are not more generous with their use of it. Dance can reinterpret the old truth that despair never comes because the going is hard, but because it is meaningless.[7]

Using children. The freshness of focusing on children in Sunday morning worship is usually enthusiastically received. In the past, children were often scheduled on Sunday evenings because it was felt they were not professional enough for Sunday morning. That idea has disappeared, and children are "in" for leading in worship—especially during seasonal and family emphases.

Decor

Three questions need to be asked regarding the decor of worship.

What can be done to present decor that would permanently enhance worship? This question is immensely important for those church facilities built in long, rectangular fashions with heavy immovable pulpits. Chancels in such churches are often high, with choir lofts that snuggle underneath vaulting rows of organ

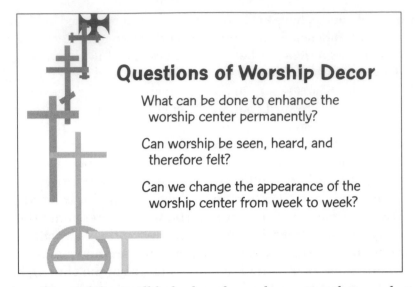

Questions of Worship Decor

What can be done to enhance the worship center permanently?

Can worship be seen, heard, and therefore felt?

Can we change the appearance of the worship center from week to week?

pipes. Remodeling will help, but the real question that needs to be asked is this: Outside of costly renovation, what can be done to redecorate and reorganize the structure for more casual and relational services?

Of particular importance in redesign is the issue of lighting and sound. Often, older sanctuaries are dimly lit and impossible to hear in. All that can be done to wake the senses should be. Setting up with better light or audio is one possibility. But setting up the sanctuary with special banners or focus centers is another option to spiritually inspire people, even as the worshipers enter the sanctuary.

This older type architecture is a painful reminder that churches were once built for monologue sermons and formal liturgy. The marketplace worship of today is best enhanced by facilities that gather a focus for dialogue, reason, and, above all, fellowship. Long, square, "high-pulpited" sanctuaries seem to package congregations for rebuke and remonstrance.

Can worship be seen, heard, and felt? Remember, television is the bright medium. Also, light and sound envelop modern theatergoers; slanted floors, staggered theater seats, elevated stages, and light and sound characterize our day. Older sanctuaries may not be able to rearrange the gothic accoutrements that speak of the dignity of God, but often it is possible to add lighting and sound systems that will enhance the services for all. Lights say, "I can see," and a good audio system says, "I can hear God." What people have to strain to hear and see rarely moves them spiritually.

Can we change the appearance of the worship center from week to week to accent a sense of variation in worship? This question is perhaps the most vital issue of decor. From Sunday to Sunday, as the flock enters the sanctuary, they should encounter a visual invitation to worship. Bouquets should come and go, banners too! With a little thoughtfulness, the sanctuary can appear ever changed and newly decorated.

Worship should be a bit like a play. Just as you can't use the same scenery for *Oklahoma* that you would for *South Pacific*, should you use the same stage for communion that you would for a service on the Christian home?

It might be helpful to think of the sanctuary as the worship theater and treat it accordingly as we prepare for each new worship experience.

At the church where I was once pastor, we had a cross we almost always put out on special communion Sundays. Sometimes we stood it up and draped the cross beam. Sometimes we laid it across the communion table. Sometimes we hung it on near-invisible wires from the ceiling. Sometimes we would feature it with a basin and pitcher. Sometimes we would have a Roman soldier bring it down the aisle. Occasionally, we would begin such services by the actual driving of a nail into the cross. Often we would lay it flat and adorn it with lighted candles. But on those Sundays when we used it, we rarely used it the same way twice in a row.

Our church had three theater drops in the ceiling where we could drop minimal theater appliances into the church on special seasons. We also had two rotating stage pivots where we could change the side altars for various worship effects. These appliances can be built cheaply, and plans for them usually abound in theater craft books.

The point in all of this is that just the decor of the worship center can and should be changed from week to week to suggest a freshness and variety in worship.

Conclusion

This chapter is a summons to the marketplace church to find a dynamic worship style that packages the marketplace sermon with interest and clout. The main agenda of those who lead in worship is to remember that the tone is to be in the Vulgate, always within the reach of people. The church's music, and other worship support forms, must play their part to enhance worship priority and impact. Finally, of course, the church, its altar, and its furniture must have an ever-changing intrigue that engages the interest of worshipers even before the service starts.

The Image-Driven Sermon 6

Our culture is addicted not only to audio but to loud audio! We are the "sound-bludgeoned" heritors of this new revolution in sound. Much of our ability to keep people's interest has to do with projection. We have almost come to the place where our sermons connote authority by decibel. The louder we talk, within reason, the more the audience focuses their attention to listen. So, to be heard is the first component of communication.

Projection

Projection is a quality of voice that varies with the mood of the speaker. The passion he or she feels in delivery requires physical energy to keep the voice level turned up over thirty minutes. Immense. This energy is easily stolen by the stress of the communicative event. Also, a night of sleeplessness can steal energy from the voice level. Saturday night often tends to be the night when the pastor is called out to adjudicate and counsel. These middle-of-the-night calls can severely injure the pastor's involvement in worship because they steal both time and stamina. Shrugging off our involvement in the crisis and getting quickly back to sleep is difficult; so personal effort must be applied just to overcome our fatigue.

Mood and passion also get involved. Sometimes church politics or the constantly circling barrage of congregational criticisms steals our vitality. It is hard to get excited about our sermon after we have just been told the personnel committee is deferring our not-so-annual raise again. The only way I know to overcome this "soul drag" is through maintaining the spiritual disciplines.

As for the issue of passion, different Sundays of the year bear different degrees of excitement. Easter usually calls for resurrection exuberance. That necessary but uninspiring sermon we must preach on financial faithfulness, however, does not stir us with as violent a passion. As our passion, so our projection. When the lightning isn't there for any particular subject, we will have to remember to push the thunder. What needs to be said must always have enough volume to be heard.

Crowd size is that factor of projection that I struggle with the most. The truth is, all of us preach bigger to bigger crowds. This is a particular problem for preachers who must constantly preach to crowds of different sizes. For the last twenty years of my life, I generally preached in a rather large church. At those times when I ministered to small congregations, I found myself terrified at the smallness. Small crowds give you only a few distinct faces, which heightens your fear that you may not be able to hold their rapt attention. Big crowds give you so many faces that there are fewer faces to intimidate you directly. Large crowds generally look at you—small crowds actually see you. Further, because of our success conditioning, we think that what we say to large crowds is of large importance and what we say to small crowds is of small importance.

Keep the sermon comfortably hearable. Shouting is not a way to emphasize, nor is it real projection. Shouts are often as unintelligible as whispers. Never assault or strain the listeners' ears. Have something to say (content) and say it with adequate force (intent). To drop either the content or the intent of the sermon is to kill the communicative process.

Rock Music Robust

Along with projection, let's speak briefly of robust speech. If we use today's society as a model, rock music (the number one choice of music for people under forty years of age) is robust as well as

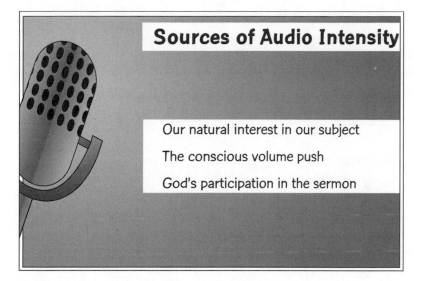

Sources of Audio Intensity

Our natural interest in our subject

The conscious volume push

God's participation in the sermon

loud. By robust I am speaking of its intensity. Loud is one thing, a commanding intensity is another.

The best way to explain this may be an examination of cinema sound tracks. There was a day when strings and reeds provided an emotive call to moviegoers to feel their way into the drama of the film. But generally these days, a more virile rock beat and heavy percussion say at every tense moment of drama, Pay attention, look alive, catch your breath—the speech and impact of this story demands it.

Most of us now are so accustomed to these robust sound tracks that the old "strings-and-reeds" sound tracks, while audible, are neither virile nor commanding.

This intensity will rise from a triple source. The first of these sources is our natural interest in our subject. Our understanding of the importance of our subject is critical. If we don't believe our subject is important to congregational understanding, the percussion of what we are saying will quickly fade to strings and reeds.

Second, our projection will come from our conscious, never-to-be-forgotten push. We, like a Shakespearean actor, must always push sound. I am not implying that we push a phony God-voice at them, but that we remember that conscious effort must always be a part of the delivery mechanism.

Finally, the most obvious source of robust vitality will come from the Holy Spirit's participation in the sermon. What God inspires will lack neither intensity nor volume. There is a trumpet-like quality of every true herald that says the urgency of what I am saying is of God.

The Audio Side of the Sermon

Audio may capture our attention in two ways. One is in the familiar strain of elevator music. This kind of audio system rarely captures or holds our attention for long. Concert music, the second way audio captures our attention, is the kind of music that focuses us powerfully. The concert is a place where we expect not so much to overhear music in the background, but to focus entirely on what the musicians on stage are doing. The sermon must, of course, fall into the concert category.

In attempting to use the ear ("faith cometh by hearing" [Rom. 10:17 KJV]) to stimulate the mind's eye, we still have to create an audio reach. The audio reach becomes an audio grasp when the listeners move forward in their pews. This is all a purely psychological ploy. Obviously, the inch or two that they lean forward does not really move them any closer to the speaker in terms of their ability to hear. It is, however, the body speaking; it is a movement of attention and intensity.

The audio reach is what the audience is doing bodily to say, "I am enthralled; I don't want to miss this." This audio reach is obvious when husbands lean over to wives (and vice versa) whispering, "What did she say? What did she say?" It is obvious also when there will be, especially among older people, an odd cocking of the ear in the pulpit's direction.

This audio reach can be created by the use of dynamics in voice control—the raising or lowering of the voice. Gesturing, too, which varies from relaxed to intense, creates this reach, styling the sermon between the forthright statement of a precept and the suspense of an unresolved story.

Vital content will keep the audio reach at optimum magnetism because it does two things. First, it says I am both talking and saying something. It is rare in sermons when both of these activities occur simultaneously. Second, it says that what I am saying is important to you. Vital is one step up from relevant. To say a sermon, or part of a sermon, is relevant means that it applies to the listener. To say it is vital means that it is all-important to the listener. When preaching fits into this last category, the audio reach becomes automatic.

The Video Side of the Sermon

The second word that characterizes our day is the word *video*. Perhaps more than any other generation, ours has been the generation of the *eye*. That being the case, we have seen all sorts of new art forms evolving from the video world: cinematography, teleplays, holograms, and so forth.

David Buttrick, in his book *Homiletic*, talks about moves and structures as the foundation of the sermon. These moves and structures may be an excellent way to begin visualizing the video part of our sermon presentation. The idea is that a sermon moves by forming structures and moving through them or forming itself around other structures and moving on. This continual movement might be symbolized by celluloid film moving over a white carbon arc to put a story on the theater screen. Remember, "movies" is a nickname for "moving pictures"—the symbol of good communication in our day. If sermons are both moving and pictorial, then cinematography, with its fast-pace interest, has come to church.

There is much to be said for the narrative theology movement in our own time. This movement is leading us to think in images even as we speak to congregations. More and more preachers who want to capture an audience and hold them are going to have to use images. They are going to have to transmit those images within the oral medium of the sermon. Preachers are going to need to think in pictures to learn to transmit them.

In this sense, the word *projection* has come to be set against the word *radio*. Once the word *radio* was the big word and our whole world orientation was audio. But now, perhaps, the big word is *video*. We have the idea that images are born on the screen of the mind.

When image and soul are coupled, they bring the kind of communication I am advocating in this chapter. Sermons will become more and more powerful as preaching is born in pictures. Image communication may very well be the key to great preaching in the future.

Picture Preaching

Image-driven preaching has very little to do with our way of preaching and more to do with our way of seeing. As hard as it may be to teach people how to preach, I believe that it will be even harder to teach people to see.

The video sermon must borrow from the video world. The devices at televised sporting events or even in the cinema are relatively simple. There are the many ways that video crews and cinematographers help us see: They *slow the motion, stop the motion,* or *speed the motion,* by "frame clicking" it through the cameras of our own living eye. They do this so that we will not just watch a progression of images but actually see them. To preach in pictures will require this same set of techniques.

Slow Motion

First, good preaching slows the motion. Here and there we must take such precepts as "Children obey your parents" (Eph. 6:1 NIV) and be sure that we slow down the precept by setting it in pictures. The phrase itself, spoken rapidly, will not evoke a picture. So we touch the slow motion button on the side of the sermon. Now, into the rapid, we'll introduce a particular story of a dysfunctional family with a particular disobedient child. Now the brakes are on and the action is slow. They who only glanced at the fast-moving precept now study it. The action and logic of the sermon is slowed down in the lengthened time span, and *a picture is born.* A second slow motion picture may be inserted from a corroborating passage in Proverbs, and while the pictures move slowly through the sermonic projection system, the account of Martin Luther's abusive childhood is added in. Now the fast pace

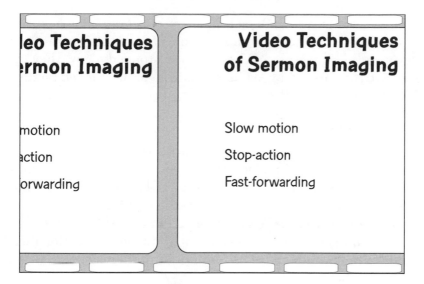

leo Techniques rmon Imaging	Video Techniques of Sermon Imaging
motion	Slow motion
ction	Stop-action
orwarding	Fast-forwarding

of a simple nonpictorial Bible precept has been seen because the pace is slowed with pictures.

Stop-Action

Second, the motion may be stopped altogether to insert a stop-action image. The Rose Bowl video crew does this regularly to show the audience why the referee called the play as he did. Here also the winner of the Kentucky Derby is stopped by a photo finish, and we see in a single frame of film that "Good Fortune" really did win; we couldn't tell he was winning while we only looked at the race. But in the stop-action film, we could clearly see he did.

Let us take the Bible precept, "Teach us to number our days, that we may apply our hearts unto wisdom" (Ps. 90:12 KJV). These words fly by without evoking a picture. So we stop the motion and offer a single image: Our offering is a painting in the Prado called *Saturn Eating His Children,* by Goya. The action stops, we describe the painting. We can take all the time we need, for the action is stopped. We can casually lead the congregation on a walk around the painting. We can give their mental eye a series of little pictures that describe the scene.

In this dark work, the ghoulish god of time holds a headless human torso in his hand; he is in the very act of eating a person. Saturn's other name is *chronos* or time. Time is always the great devourer of all who live. The action is stopped—now they can see. Are they just seeing a Goya painting in the stopped picture? No, they are seeing Psalm 90:12.

Fast-Forwarding

In terms of movement, most sermons suffer from bulky inertia. The third way of making them see, therefore, may be most appealing: We give them the pictures in fast-forward so that they are forced to pay attention to be sure the rapid-fire incoming images are not missed. When cinema gets draggy, the art of the cinematographers begins an onslaught of images—fractionalized seconds of fast-forward. The pictures hurl themselves at us too quickly to be ignored.

In sermons, fast-forwarding images may be done not by using whole stories but by using bits of stories. For instance, in your sermon you may define sin as missing the mark—the ultimate morality that God had planned for us. Sin is:

Hitler's Aryan pride
Hefner's sexism of ego
Hussein's swaggering threats
Hirohito's bogus godhood
Herod's massacre of Christians

Notice that in this fast series of pictures all the images are real historical icons. But the list could as easily have been taken from fiction. Sin is:

Hans Solo's arrogance
Hester Prynne's silence
Hans Brinker's presumption
Hansel's compliance
Hamlet's brusque treatment of his mother

When pictures are being thrown at an audience, it is best not to mix fiction and nonfiction. Mixing the real and imaginary images gives a feeling of lost credibility to the whole thing.

Another way of fast-forwarding images is a rapid use of concise phrases. Sin is:

Hypocrisy in religious practice

Hawking pearls at an auction of swine

Helping yourself to the treasure hidden in the field

Holding back the truth we're called to preach

Hitching your wagon to a star while compromising your ethics

The glitch lies not in using these devices to help others see but in first seeing the images ourselves. It is this part of the video sermon that is almost impossible to teach. Seeing what we look at and saving what we see precedes preaching in pictures. Jesus was perhaps warning us of the difficulty of saving these images when he said, "Do you have eyes but fail to see?" (Mark 8:18 NIV).

For me, taking up watercolor caused me to see form and image like I had not done before. If my use of pictures has become more crisp in my sermons, it may be that watercolor first taught me how to see in pictures so I could later preach in them. Photography could perform the same function for someone else. So would learning art appreciation. So would reviewing movie or television productions for a local newspaper. But if none of these things suit you, perhaps an interest in fiction, theater, or film can serve you in a less direct way. In these less involved media, the eye of the novelist or playwright still catches and holds the image for us.

Losing and Regaining Audience Togetherness

Throughout the rest of this book I will have much to say about keeping audience interest, but for the moment let us focus on the ebb and flow of listener attention.

A four-step process moves us away from the sermonizer. When we are all bound together by a tight intensity of good visual or video stimulation, the picture-sermon may be assaulting us pri-

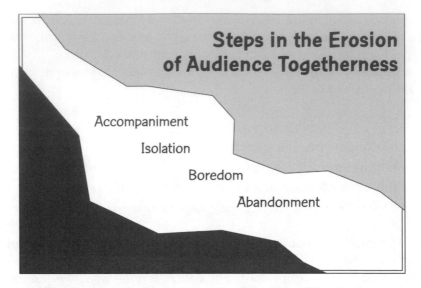

marily in graphic fashion; but when we are all locked together on (perhaps even riveted to) what a speaker is saying, I like to call this first stage *accompaniment*. In this accompaniment stage of fastening to the audio, we move with the speaker toward the conclusion that he or she might wish to direct us.

From this positive stage, however, we can move to the second stage: *isolation*. This is the point in which the sermon either becomes too dull to attend to or we, for some other reason, are distracted and move away from accompanying the speaker to isolating ourselves. Once we have separated from the content, we reach stage three, which is *boredom*. Then finally, of course, our minds stray to other things and we reach *abandonment*. In this final step, we have moved as far as we can from the audio side of the sermon. Here we abandon the speaker altogether.

Correcting a sermon's straying course must be done while it is being preached. Great preachers keep themselves flexible enough to work the alienating four-step process in reverse as well; that is, they are able to amend the delivery of the sermon so that they halt the erosion of audience interest in process.

The four stages of togetherness in all public speaking begin with the most desirable state: accompaniment. *Accompaniment* means that our listeners are "with us." We are in the sermon to-gether. There is dialogue. As preachers, our words are spoken. Their words are all body language: the nod of the head, the glint of the eye, the earnest jaw, the fingernail between the teeth, the attentive leaning in our direction.

If the audience loses this intensity they move to *isolation*. At this stage our lack of sermon relevance or our stodgy style has allowed them to drift. Here some adjustment must be made to draw them back. It may mean we have to scroll the sermon outline quickly ahead in our mind. This will allow us to come quickly to the next, more interesting point. It may mean a hasty termination if the sermon is nearing its unriveting end. It may mean "Plan B" or the insertion of an illustration that will get them back before they step to *boredom*, where it's harder to get them back because it's harder for them to want to come back. If they reach *abandonment*, all is lost, because at this stage all sermonic dialogue is over. Their spirits have at this stage left the service; only their bodies remain in attendance.

Obviously, to check the erosion process before accompaniment atrophies to abandonment means the development of a highly flexible style of communication. Manuscript sermon readers are often lost to all hope when this occurs. An extemporaneous style, however, can artfully dodge and pirouette back into the inspiring center of our lost togetherness. To keep them listening is basic; no truth or content—however lofty or noble—sails across the abyss of disinterest. We must quickly give our listeners strong, crisp images to get us back to the accompaniment stage again.

Battling Sermon Decay

If people lose interest because they can't "see" our argument (the erosion of the pictorial sermon), they will also lose interest because the audio function goes dead. The first and most important stage of losing our audio togetherness is the *slippage of content*. This is obviously the hardest part of the sermon to amend in process. On our feet, trying to invent the stuff of argument can only be done after years of dedicated reading and studying. A shallow academic life will be useless at this point.

A second and more easily corrected loss of audio interest is related to a *slippage of passion*. Passion comes from the intensity of our involvement in our subject. If we notice the interest of our subject slipping, it is usually a simple matter of impersonating the energy. While the best energy comes from the force of our convictions about the importance of our subject, there is a certain sense in which energy can be hyped, thus giving a *sui generis* intensity to what we are saying.

Step three, a *loss of volume* in projection usually follows close on the heels of a diminished passion. This stage of erosion is deadly because lowered volume creates a deaf audience. What they can't hear cannot be corrected at all. Immediate and forced projection is the only hope. But we need to remember that volume without content equals noise. Loud *with* content, however, equals force. As volume joins meaning, content will build intrigue, and intrigue can be restored to the sleepy in dialogue.

Stage four, *isolation*, then occurs. All audience togetherness ceases. The entire crowd becomes separated from each other and from the speaker as well. The last stage is *jettison*. All of this occurs because the audio side of the sermon is neglected. Paul's adage that faith comes by hearing has a corollary truth: Disbelief is the product of a soundless sermon. It is a musical with no soundtrack—an electrical storm without thunder.

A Final Examination

Once the preacher reaches the magic place of joining good projection to strong content, real motivation is born. And when intrigue and motivation are wed, the result is authority. While *authority* has become a kind of dirty word in this day of the indicative sermon, there is still much to be said for the combination of intrigue and motivation. This authority leaves the audience open to the conclusions the speaker has drawn. The pastor can then motivate the audience toward the scriptural agenda for the hour. We need not abandon authority because it seems irreverent and irrelevant. It is always important to remember that Jesus was once praised because he taught as one having authority and not like the scribes.

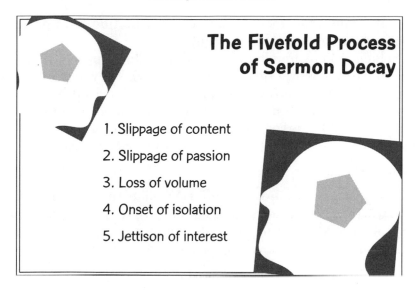

The Fivefold Process of Sermon Decay

1. Slippage of content
2. Slippage of passion
3. Loss of volume
4. Onset of isolation
5. Jettison of interest

Essential Elements of the Video Sermon

Four things are essential to the video sermon.

Preaching Image, Not Plot

The video sermon means that we are primarily interested in preaching image and not plot. In this entertainment generation, most would agree that in a world where so many new novels and screenplays are being written, image has generally surpassed plot in storytelling. Image survives in every theater. Whatever the story line is, we generally remember the images. In narrative preaching, the sermon generally stops to say, "I may be telling you a story that you have heard before; nonetheless, pay attention. As you listen I will create new images for your minds that will help you apprehend the important content of my sermon."

Selling Vision

Imaginative sermons create visionary listening, and vision fans the imagination into flames. In a building program, pictures of a new building encourage the congregation to build. Likewise, the video sermon always sells image. Image as a way of seeing ourselves allows us more concrete self-definition than perceptual and logical teaching ever could.

Selling vision is much different than selling image. "Without a vision, the people perish" (Prov. 29:18 KJV). They might not actually perish in a church service, but they will certainly nod off! Vision answers their need for meaning by asking them two vital questions: "What is your image or picture of God's great plan for the world?" and "How do you picture your part in this plan?"

Selling Image

Image and vision certainly differ. Vision is the overall picture into which we fit our lives. Image is how we see ourselves within that picture. Many of today's most popular preachers have succeeded because they have sold people a vision that allowed their hearers to see themselves as ultimately rich and successful. But these preachers have also succeeded because they encouraged their hearers to hunger after an improved self-image. This new mental image was one in which listeners saw themselves in a particular way that enhanced all of life.

Selling image is different than selling vision. Vision comes as they answer the question of what they should be doing or where they should be going in life. Selling image asks, "Who are you? How do you appear? How do you see yourself as you move along this pilgrimage toward fulfilling God's ultimate vision for your life?"

Packaging

The most effective delivery comes double-packaged in *tight preparation* and *loose delivery.* I will discuss tight preparation more fully later, but for the moment let me describe it as a closely edited sermon manuscript. This closely edited document will contain both a cogent outline and polished logic. The language of sermon artistry will be there too. We must then add to this manuscript a "hang loose" delivery that is characterized by both a relational style and an inductive conversational mystique. In the tension between tight preparation and casual delivery, the glory of the marketplace sermon is born.

I think that the final point of the video side of the sermon means that great marketplace communicators must learn to package meaning. When they leave the services week after week, people must be able to say, "I understand image, for here is how I see myself," and "I understand vision, for here is how I see God's purposes." They came to us in the hope of catching some liberating vision of themselves. The audio-video sermon can furnish them with a meaningful new self-image in which they will become more central to the vision of their ultimate use to God.

Crafting the Marketplace Sermon 7

Marketplace preachers writing marketplace sermons must understand the marketplace generation. How do career ad-persons arrive at artistry and clout in marketing? The average television commercial blazes with staccato-fire images. Visuals fly at us so fast they seem doubled back upon one another. There are dissolve fades, slow motions, freeze frames, and fast forward sections of film. There are full color and black-and-white eye bombardments. And the expertise of hundreds of people go into the making of a single television film. In the preparation of the marketplace sermon, artistry is key, and so in this chapter let us examine the components of that artistry.

The Scripture

The week-to-week preaching of the Bible will furnish people with a stabilizing hermeneutic as they search for clues to interpret life. Elizabeth Achtemeier defined an Old Testament Prophet as one who knew where and when and why God was at work in the world.[1] But it is the week-to-week issues of what we are to say and how we are to say it that consume our study.

What Version of the Bible?

This question is more crucial than it might seem. Marketplace auditors want the Bible to be readable and relevant. They want these ancient words to feel as contemporary as the morning news. Along with the Living Bible and the Contemporary English Version, I want to recommend Eugene Peterson's *The Message*. Many modern listeners will respond readily to such new versions and paraphrases. While many of the best preachers know and use the Greek and Hebrew texts in their sermon preparation, to many, Greek and Hebrew words will move the sermon to a place too long-ago-and-far-away from the world they inhabit.

How to Read It?

How we read the text is of far more significance than the question of which version. The question of how to read a text should have as its most immediate answer "effectively."

The issue of what makes a reader effective always begins with creative oral interpretation. Sermon texts may be creatively interpreted in many ways. For instance, they may be made to come alive by using a solo reader who reads in a dramatic style but without ostentation. Such a solo reader may present the text even more dramatically by memorizing it and interpreting it theatrically. Many of the Psalms, the Lord's Prayer, 1 Corinthians 13, and a host of other passages have musical settings that can be sung in dramatic fashion.

Another option is to have two or three readers jointly present a text. A theater of readers can be used to read quite effectively. In certain narrative texts, a single reader might read while mimes or tableau actors act out the narrative being read. Indeed, there are so many ways it might be done that one wonders why preachers give so little attention to the matter. Often, they stand mumbling textual majesty in monotones. Such poor handling of God's Word must at least be a sin against the Holy Spirit, who, in such poor reading, finds it hard to get a word in edgewise. Further, such poor reading implies, "As soon as I get God's boring but necessary Word out of the way, we'll get to my really exciting stuff." Frederick Buechner hits the nail on the head when he describes the preacher's stepping up to the pulpit and turning on the little light that illumines his sermon.[2] Truly, the stakes are high! There are those present coping with all kinds of sin! There are also those present who are contemplating suicide, embezzlement, and any number of desperate solutions. They are starving to get God's light on their decision-making. The emotional struggle is so intense that we dare not read God's Word poorly.

Selecting the Wide Passage

Often, more of the Scripture should be read than is needed by the sermon exposition. This contextualizes the text and provides listeners with a means of correlating sermon facts with the Bible as a whole—or at least with the larger background from which the text is drawn.

The Text and the Topical Series

Because the topical expositor needs to be the model for attracting the seeker to the church, should a series of sermons ever be based on a single passage? How true Ron Allen's counsel is: "The Christian community has consistently found that it comes into a fresh, vital relationship with God when it gathers around the Bible, and engages the Bible in the light of Christian tradition, keeps in touch with its own experience, and reasons its way to a sensible understanding of the text."[3] Doesn't this truth mandate a sermon series? The answer is an obvious yes. But hear this caution: The short topical series will stand in bold preference to a long series of sermons drawn from something like the Apocalypse or the Gospel of Matthew. By long, I generally mean anything beyond eight or ten sermons. In my best judgment, a topical series should include somewhere from two to five sermons.

A series on marriage might easily find this amount of topics from 1 Corinthians alone. The Song of Solomon might also provide fertile soil for such a series. I have four sermons on the foundation of the Christian home all drawn out of Genesis 1–3. I have four sermons on servanthood all drawn out of Philippians 2. I have a series on developing your inner life all drawn from 1 Corinthians 1–9, and another on six key aspects of leadership all taken from the life of King David.

Also, nothing is wrong with developing a series of topical sermons drawn from widely separate passages. The balance always has to be weighed between finding the best single passage whose exposition defines the topic or several consecutive passages that may better define the series. If at all possible, I like finding correlated passages that allow me to move through a single body of Scripture as a close comment on several related topics. The reason for this is that, in a single block of text, the hearers can best remember and correlate from week to week.

Enhancing the Text

However the text is presented, the sermon may be drawn from a particularly difficult section of Scripture; if so, it will be necessary to comment on the text, giving the audience the additional information they need to understand the passage. Elizabeth Achtemeier is arguing for enhancing the text when she reminds us that we set every Old Testament story sermon against a vast congregational ignorance. She is also arguing that the story of Moses on Sinai should be allowed to stack their mental library with sound teaching.[4] Nonetheless the point is well made that most of the church attenders need a little help bridging their secular world to the biblical world, about which they know nothing. Anything obscure that dulls a congregational understanding of the passage should be treated so thoroughly that their misunderstandings are eliminated before the sermon begins. The same worship resources we called for in interpreting the text can be used here. Dramatists, children's choirs, deaf choirs can all be drawn in to help illuminate the passage.

Picking the Focal Passage

From the wider text the selection of a narrower passage should be made. It is best to give the audience only a single verse, or better yet, a portion of a single verse as the focal passage. James Black says:

> Out of the wide text a narrower passage should be selected but it should be done in such a way as to make the entire book and single passage speak as one. The key thing is to be sure that enough study has gone into the passage to make it speak.[5]

Never forget that the sermon's only point should be encapsulated within the focal passage. Other passages should be used to illustrate or make clear the focal text and its single sermonic point. Whenever possible, always use correlating Scriptures to illustrate the focal text. Let Scripture speak to Scripture. Use easier parts of the Bible to illustrate the more difficult parts. But be careful in this. The single point of the sermon should *never* be broadened to include other ideas. The marketplace mind will respond best to a tight, nonrambling, single-focus presentation.

Obtaining the Sermon Logo

The final reduction of the text (again best done before the sermon) is the sermon logo. The sermon logo is a one- to seven-word phrase that states the theme of the sermon. This phrase or word may be repeated often so that the logo lodges near the center of the sermon argument and remains central in the exegesis as other supporting arguments come and go.

One other thing that should be applied to the contemporaneity of worship is the sermon objective. Harold Bryson says that this sermon objective should be able to be written out in fifteen words or less.[6] It would indeed be a happy wedding of worship and preaching if worship leaders would apply a single sentence objective of what they want contemporary worship to accomplish. The same sentence that defines the sermon should define the worship as well.

How does all of this work? How do the wider passage, the focal passage, and the sermon logo all relate? Let me illustrate with two or three of my own sermons. I have a sermon on servanthood called "The Mind of a Servant." Here's how the various categories could be named:

1. The wider passage—Philippians 2:1–8
2. The enhancer—I preface this sermon with a brief explanation of the emptying process of Christ in the incarnation. I explain to the people that this passage is the highest celebration of Christ in a single passage in the New Testament.
3. The focal passage—Philippians 2:5 This passage focuses on the topic.
4. The sermon logo—(from Philippians 2:5 KJV) "Let This Mind Be in You"

As a second example, I have a sermon called "Dying in Moab"; the sermon focuses on Moses' dying outside of Canaan.

1. The wider passage—Deuteronomy 34:1–8
2. The enhancer—I explain how, in Numbers 20:1–11, Moses is commanded to touch the rock, but in a temper tantrum he thrashes the rock and so he is allowed to see the promised land in Deuteronomy 34 but *not* allowed to cross over to it.
3. The focal passage—Deuteronomy 34:5
4. The sermon logo—(from Deuteronomy 34:5) "Dying in Moab"; the repetition of this single idea is used to encourage the listeners again and again. We must always be faithful and never let a loss of self-control become a blight on God's future use of our lives.

The logo supplies focus and direction. The entire process is necessary to the preparation of every sermon we preach. We must not forget that single-theme preaching keeps a single orientation and direction while at the same time remaining correlated to the whole text.

The Polishing

Polishing means adding the sparkle that makes the worshipers *enjoy* the sermon even as they listen to it. The development of sparkle and charm in the sermon will require some manuscripting. It is not possible to develop a polished extemporaneous sermon without adding to our preparation the precision of writing as a craft.

Crafting

Adding sparkle to the sermon cannot be done without the hard work of crafting the sermon. Although I argued earlier for the manuscripting of the entire sermon, I realize that most busy pastors are not going to yield to this all-consuming discipline. But what is the minimal amount of manuscripting that must be done? Again, since sparkle has to do with the artistry of using words, total spontaneity must be abandoned in favor of the writing out at least of some parts of the sermon. Robert McNeil wrote of his upbringing: "My mother would weep over a book, my father would lose himself in one for hours . . . all this combined to fashion a childhood which made words important. . . . Dickens was the first writer I met who could make a small person laugh or cry. . . . His words show in themselves that language is constantly dashing out to change its wardrobe."[7] Sermons, too, must yearn for crafting that makes words "dress up" to do their best work for God. The caveat that must be sounded is this: Writing any part of the sermon may tempt us to read back to the audience the fruit of our clever crafting. This urge must be avoided, and it is difficult (and to some degree, perhaps a bit phony) to try to appear to have spontaneously spoken what we have labored long to achieve.

How much should be written? It depends on the occasion. A sermon prepared for a highly professional crowd should be mostly written—especially if on this single sermon rests much of our career or reputation. But even for less auspicious occasions, introductions, conclusions, key stories, and illustrations should all be written. Care should always be taken to avoid ostentatious language that calls attention to itself. But narrative nuances and scintillating phrases will not only make that immediate story interesting to our hearers, over a period of time the struggle will develop in us the art of polished storytelling.

Jokes or the Light Relief

Except for the highly skilled ecclesiastical comedian, jokes are risky business. They are dangerous for several reasons.

First of all, they have usually been around for awhile; a joke previously heard deflects the sermonic interest away from the topic. It leaves the hearer trying to remember when he or she heard it the first time and how better or worse it was told on that occasion. Second, they are usually used more to hold attention than to illustrate the subject. Third, jokes have a way of trivializing a serious argument. Finally, if they are corny, they reflect either on the preacher's intellect or judgment or both.

Those who have some ability to tell jokes must always run the risk of having people miss the punch line. Having to say, "but se-

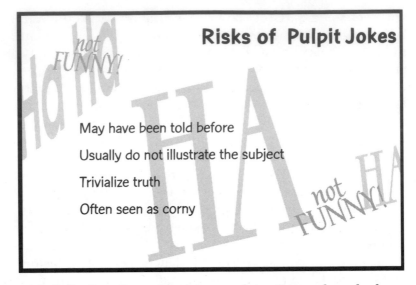

riously folks," is often a blushing apology. Even when the humor does apply to the subject, the laughter is often spotty. Most of all, the jesting pulpiteer often appears uncomfortable with the medium of joke-telling. To the skilled jesting pulpiteer I can easily say—Bully! But to the rest of us, we need to hear this caveat: The only thing worse than boring a congregation is embarrassing them.

Better than telling jokes is learning to use anecdotes and stories that have a creative lightness about them. Humor is a tension-breaker and an interest-grabber. It should be spaced within the arid places in the sermon to eliminate dragging dullness. But developing a narrative that makes a place for lightness requires a keen mind or the willingness to manuscript those passages in a sermon that will carry the lightness.

One further warning: In a day of multiculturalism, *never* include ethnic slurs or overtones of dialect. It is totally improper to offend even one person in an attempt to get laughter from the other ninety-nine in attendance.

The Art of Being Oneself

Nothing enhances authenticity (and sparkle) like the art of being ourselves. Professional comedians generally succeed on this very basic principle. Our unique personhood adds polish, flair, and above all, light to the presentation.

One of the things that so often befuddles uniqueness in proclamation is that so many preachers adopt a stage or pulpit voice. This usually is a sonorous and sanctified voice they assume will add authority and mystique to their sermons. The real truth is that it defeats and destroys the sermon's sparkle and charm. Our best qualities only come through when we preach unafraid to be our real selves.

I know a pastor who is the most humorous of souls in ordinary conversation. He is known colloquially as a "stitch"! But when he preaches, this warm, humorous, congenial person is obscured by the demeanor of the serious martyr, seeking mystic, and severe scholar that he thinks he ought to be. How much sparkle might come to his sermon if he only realized that the most scintillating definition of preaching is "truth communicated through personality."

Synonym Sifting

In my book *Spirit, Word, and Story,* I dedicated a lot of space to this form of sermon crafting. The idea behind synonym sifting means that we are searching for just the right word that most strongly carries an idea. For instance, the word *glad* is weaker than the word *joyous,* which is weaker than the word *rapturous.* Why say *fine* when you can say *splendid;* or *sweet* when you can say *sugarcoated? Succulent* is better than *savory,* which is better than *tasty. Pretty* is weaker than *beautiful,* which is weaker than *resplendent.*[8]

To grow adept at synonym sifting again requires manuscripting. Context and beauty are two aspects in sermon construction. Nothing will suffice for a lack of content in a sermon, but those who learn to couple ornament and logic will find that they possess oratorical sway. Aquinas was a natural at this; so was Peter Marshall. Among current preachers Walt Wangerin, Frederick Buechner, and Will Willimon stand out clearly as role models of the art.

Ian Pitt-Watson once told me that the art of ornamentation is an arduous art that depends on a freshness of mind and a disciplined lifetime of practice. "The more tired I am when I preach, the more mundane are the words that come to inhabit my sermons," he said. "When my fatigue is severe enough, only weak words come, and weak words put together make weak sermons." Bruce Salmon says that sermon stories should develop suspense.[9] Weak words will not tell strong stories. And poorly chosen words will not build intrigue.

Borrowing Interest and Style

Much of the sparkle that adorns the delivery of the sermon will rise spontaneously from the natural interests of the marketplace preacher. In the paragraphs above, we talked about sparkle coming from the attractive demeanor of being ourselves. In my philosophy of preaching, I encourage the preacher to create interest around the sermon by appealing to the "preacher's habitat." The world of our own natural interests (our habitat) becomes the matrix from which we draw the audience toward us by using these irresistible elements of our interests.

Maximizing Your Habitat

How do we maximize our habitat to enrich preaching? The weakness of suggesting this is that it encourages us to thrust ourselves into our preaching. David Buttrick warns the preacher against every mention of the self. Still, the marketplace sermon is one form that, more than all others, makes friends on an interpersonal basis. This mandates a conservative thrusting of ourselves and our habitat into the sermon.

Harry Emerson Fosdick once referred to preaching as "counseling on a group basis." Success in counseling always runs the risk of self-disclosure and the risky overexhibition of our living and interest. The key is that we disclose our personal lifestyle as we touch upon some very large truth. Then the casual mention of our personal interests juxtaposed to great truths will be slight.

I enjoy the world of art. I readily and frequently disclose this in my preaching. I have a sermon built around my first encounter with the work of Van Gogh. His *Potato Eaters* profoundly impacted me with his love of the poor. When I consider his years as a minister to miners I am touched that he immortalized the common people—maybe this is what incarnation is all about. At least I sermonize his art in such a way. I remain casual and unimportant in telling the truth I want to illustrate. It would be wrong if I puffed up my abilities as an art critic or bragged that I had seen more original Wyeths than any preacher west of the Mississippi.

Let us take a friend of mine, whose habitat is a fanatic love of football. His sermon illustrations keep touch with the life he loves. Athletic competition spoons into his sermons some wonderful tales of victory, defeat, and the overcoming life. Yet his personal involvement in his illustration remains minimal. He might include himself as the spectator or the friend of a well-known athlete who illustrates some point of his sermon; but once again, the focus is never on him so much as his interest. Preaching out of one's habitat will allow the preacher to keep his or her text close to life.[10] Sermons that completely ignore the preacher's habitat get too liturgical and remote to be interesting. Such sermons smack of preachers who neglect in their sermons what consumes the natural course of their lives.

Our habitats command a style borrowed by our unique and particular use of adjectives, idioms, and ways of phrasing things. The preacher should never become an impressionist, imitating anyone else's character or authentic being. Still, it is always good to see how others use words and phrases that hold the interest of their audience. If we can authentically borrow style to add to our own uniqueness, we should do so. If, in watching others, we see how we might add class to our act, we should. But ever beware that imitation of others can result in losing the best of ourselves.

First Line, Last Line, Logo

Three items are especially important in crafting the sermon: the first line, the last line, and the logo. Dealing with the last word first, the logo should be short, memorable, and simple. Robert Schuller's book titles might make excellent logos:

Tough Times Never Last, but Tough People Do!
The Be (Happy) Attitudes

Self-Esteem: The New Reformation
When the Going Gets Tough, the Tough Get Going

This kind of statement (without the ring of cliché would be best) is the logo that encapsulates the sermon's theme. The logo may be used aloud to call the congregation back to the theme again and again (probably more than four or five times in a twenty-minute sermon is overkill); the repetition of a specially memorable logo will be quite welcome. Remember a cliché, if it is not utterly hackneyed, may serve quite well. The repetition of "I have a dream" in the famous King sermon is a splendid example of how the logo serves.

The first line and last line serve as the sermon's runways. The most dangerous times in flying are liftoff and touchdown. They are also the most precarious times in preaching. Really, it is more than an issue of first and last lines, it is an issue of first and last paragraphs, but the issue remains the same. The first and last moments of a sermon must serve well. The local pastor beginning too formally or too grandly will seem affected. H. Grady Davis, in his *Design for Preaching,* says that if we use ordinary human inventions like salesmanship and human promotion we will build only a human institution.[11] He meant this to be a criticism of where the church has come to rest. The church that is reaching outside its walls with marketplace sermons will often be using some approaches that do at first seem too secular to use in building the church of Jesus Christ. But let us not be overhasty in this assessment.

My whole purpose in this book is to endow preaching with a perspective that allows dying churches and denominations to recapture contemporary interest in their time-honored subject. Being human in our approach to the sermon and worship is the best way to build a transition between ourselves and the needy world. It is generally good to build an easy transitional mode between the sermon and the worship matrix that has come before. A compliment to the choir, a warm response to a reader or soloist, a thank-you, a pleasant "good morning"; all these establish a humanity that bridges and prepares the sermon's way.

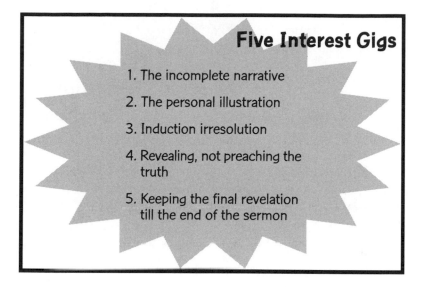

Five Interest Gigs

1. The incomplete narrative
2. The personal illustration
3. Induction irresolution
4. Revealing, not preaching the truth
5. Keeping the final revelation till the end of the sermon

Although I will touch on this later, the last line should often be left with some general and relational remark that brings the audience back into contact with the human side of the orator.

The Interest Gig

In this section, I want to deal with the use of five items that, properly employed, will keep the audience tied to our sermons. Long years ago I read where Barbara Tuchman, the historian, said that she posted a smile sign above her typewriter that read: "Will the reader turn the page?" Every great book is a page-turner. Great preaching likewise ensnares attention. The question is how do we keep people on the line; how, in a sense, do we keep them turning the pages of our argument? Every preacher with any long-term experience in the pulpit has painfully watched people shut down in the middle of his or her argument. Here are five cardinal suggestions for keeping them listening.

The Incomplete Narrative

Eugene Lowry has made one aspect of sermonic attention very clear: The way to keep people listening is not to give them the

Three Risks
of Personal Illustrations

May violate confidences

Focus too much on the speaker

Often make a speaker seem arrogant

conclusion of the argument till you reach the end of the sermon. Frequently, as Lowry lectures, he will go to the piano (he is an excellent pianist) and play a simple "do" to "ti" scale, but withholding the final "do" that closes the scale. While the entire audience waits breathlessly for him to play the final note and bring the scale to resolution, he reminds them that it is the irresolution that keeps them listening.

Lowry has perfected what he calls "Lowry's loop." Graphically, it looks like this:

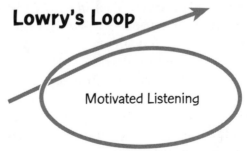

The point of the loop is the people listening while Eugene Lowry explains that single narrative preaching contains the story hook that keeps them listening. During the swale in the loop they evaluate, measure, reflect, and ready themselves to resume the upward gain of anticipation as they pull out of the swale and ready to bring the resolution to their anticipation.[12]

His argument is strong: The way to keep people listening to a tale is not to conclude the story. While stories remain unfinished, interest remains acute.

The Personal Illustration

Between sermon classicists and the more relational preachers, there is now a standing argument on the issue of using personal illustrations. Let's look at its inherent dangers before examining the positive side of this issue. The danger of personal illustrations arc three.

First, all stories involving the preacher usually involve someone else, often members of the minister's family. The preacher's children all too often wind up victims of sermonic child abuse. Wives, too, can take a psychological bludgeoning. Also, the wide world of the counseling room and the strong tales of need and suffering that serve so well to illustrate sermons abound in the life of ministers. They *do* powerfully illustrate, but these illustrations are given to the minister's use only with permission. To violate any person's dignity or confidence merely to illustrate a sermon is unconscionable. The first rule of using personal illustrations is that permission must be given by those who appear in the illustration.

Second, does the personal illustration make over the preacher so much that it deflects the sermon focus to the preacher? If the subject is obscured rather than complimented by the illustration, it should not be used.

Third, the supreme question may be, does this personal illustration make the preacher seem arrogant? Does the pulpit story seem "braggy," or is it a story that points up its lesson without pretention? A safe rule on this is to use most frequently those illustrations that show how the preacher learned (perhaps by this horrible, personal example) something in his sermon content.

There are, however, three blessings that can result from using personal illustrations. First, they are relational, conversational, and usually utterly practical. In this relational age, such preaching is a conversational plus. Personal stories and nearly all con-

Three Blessings of Personal Illustrations

Confession holds ultimate interest

Self-disclosure can break an elitist tone

The humanity of the pastor suggests the personhood of God

fessional preaching draws like a magnet. Be sure that any part of a confessional sermon confesses only the speaker's sins and not the sins of unsuspecting confidants.

Second, the personal illustration breaks through the elitist, academic, pontifical tone of the message. Second-person sermons are bossy and brash. Third-person sermons are lecturish and aloof. But the first-person type encourages conversation, since one can scarcely say "I" without saying "you." And while the "I" that has no interest in "you" amounts to sermonic arrogance, the "I" of a truly selfless pastor is a person whose other-centered life attracts. The good, healthy sermonic "I" says, "Draw up your pew and let's have a coffee-and-doughnuts communication." As we have said earlier, the word *homily* means conversation, and conversation is shared communication.

Third, and this may be the remotest shot at the subject, the theology of preaching begins and ends with the personhood of God. If God's personhood is not made obvious in the sermon, the sermon will hold no interest to the flock. The pastor makes accessible these personal attributes of God. Ian Pitt-Watson, in his gem-like *Primer* (a small but glistening book on preaching), reminds us that the "what" of our preaching is the first consideration for the sermon. The "what" is the theologically correct text.

But when the "what" of preaching is properly in place it will be personal. Every biblical book is the tale of someone's personal reaction to God. What kind of Bible would we have if Jonah hadn't mentioned himself in his sermons? Or Hosea, or Moses, or certainly, Jesus? Protecting the theological heart of sonship is important. The pastor's overfrequent inclusion of the self in the sermon will not serve. But something of the pastor's personal life as part of the ongoing life of the congregation is a powerful force indeed.

The key is to use our own lives to expand our "Thus saith the Lord" to "Thus saith the Lord to me." In this way, God's ancient word becomes his contemporary word. This all assumes that the pastor's life is in a constant state of being spiritually formed, and that he or she cares desperately about being Christlike.

Inductive Irresolution

As it is lethal to let listeners come to the end of a story before the story ends, so it is dangerous to let them make up their minds about all that the sermon is going to say before it is all said. Inductive preaching always implies that the issue of reason and conclusion is left to the listener. But if they can leap naturally ahead of your argument and reach their own conclusions before you give the information they need to decide all correctly, their need to listen will be preempted by their need to think about other issues unrelated to your argument.

A storyteller never gives away the ending. A logician never allows the members of an audience to arrive at their own conclusion before they have the facts. The argument of the sermon must move logically to the conclusion, which the entire audience reaches at the same time. Premature conclusions cut short sermon attention. They will not hold the excitement of those great inductive conclusions that motivates them to act in accord with their own self-discovery.

Revealing, Not Preaching the Truth

In the New Testament, there is a proclaiming difference between *kerusso* and *apokalupto*. *Kerusso*, or exhortation, is a blatant call, an urgent near-demand. However, indicative preaching (indeed, indicative anything) is in! Newscasters and anchor-persons unquestionably influence how we think, yet they never tell us how to think. They marshall information on their side of influence and leave it there. If we arrive at conclusions with them, it was not their command, it was only our reckoning with the facts they gave us. *Kerusso* is a marshalling word. Exhortation as a preaching style was a primary style of the nineteenth century. It has also characterized much of the evangelistic preaching of the twentieth century. But here at the threshold of the twenty-first century, it is possible that the era of the sermon that told people what to do is over.

The indicative sermon now must preach persuadingly only as it has the imperatives of God. Our "thus-saith-the-Lords" must remain in place, but they must gain their force through inductive process. Most people are not so impious that they would say aloud, "I don't care what the Lord says"; but they are in no haste to apply anybody's word to their lives—even God's—until they see its relevance and need. *Free will* now makes the sovereignty of God fully explain itself before it gives God some charge of life.

This being so, *apokalupsis* is the key to great preaching. As divine anchorpersons, preachers must spend all week marshalling the evidence for their Sunday morning argument. Then, after the anthem, they draw the curtain (for this is the basic meaning of *apokalupto*) and display the facts, the motivation, the devotion. Then it is altar time! Whether or not there is an open altar, some time should be given for the audience to internalize their reaction (or decision) to the sermon's revelation. Then the insight may come as it did to the Revelator, "And I saw heaven opened." This goal-oriented, indicative, inductive preaching does indeed open heaven. Best of all, it puts the doorknob of those golden gates in the hand of the listener, not the preacher.

Keeping the Final Revelation till the End of the Sermon

If apocalypse and insight occur, sermons, like intense dramas, will not drop the ball at the conclusion. Remember this, we are not bringing an audience to our conclusions nor to our remedy for their desperation. Every sermonizer needs to remember this: Where there is a tragedy, God has his remedy.[13] The final revelation of the sermon will then justify the collective time that all the hearers (and this can be thousands of hours or weeks, depending on the size of the church) have given the sermon. I admit my bias here for big endings. I like either anthems or sermons that have "MGM" endings. However, there are all sorts of ways of ending either anthems or sermons, from *piano* to *fortissimo.* As to the *fortissimo* ending, it is important to remember that the noise of it should not be greater than the content of it. Under the billowing smoke, there should be a worthy fire. The lightning should be equal to the thunder. As to the *piano* ending, the softness should be impact-loud—hence, eloquent. When the softness quiets the mind, some subtle but transposed revelation should occur. Some finale should be forthcoming. The delicate softness must contain a still small voice. If not, the exercise is futile. The sermon is not just soft; it is powerless.

Week by week the people should be so conditioned to high content endings that they won't slip out of services early to "beat the Methodists to the cafeteria." The final revelation consistently says, "If you leave early, you will miss the best part of this hour, for I am not accustomed to giving the goody away until I conclude."

Story endings and undrawn conclusions both grab attention, but nothing works quite like the impending feeling that a great announcement is shortly to be made! Preaching to the same congregation over a period of years gives the preacher the right to build into his or her congregation this weekly moment of terminal sermonic suspense: "Since our pastor always ends the homily with worthwhile revelation, we dare not quit listening or we'll miss the moment of apocalypse." Remember that apocalypse is not just the idea of a biblical ending. It is a biblical ending that reveals; it "draws the drapes . . . it unveils." In the secular mind, it's the "fat lady" (or to be genderly generous, the "fat man") syndrome—"It's not over till she sings," or as Yogi Berra said: "It's not over till it's over."

Paul's sermon on Mars' Hill (Acts 17) is a classic example. The Athenians listened to him down to the big revelation (the resurrection). Once the sermon apocalypse had been reached, for the most part, they rejected Paul's revelation. But they did listen down to the moment that the unveiling of the biblical doctrine occurred. The great homiletical principle included in Acts 17 is that the Athenians weren't free to decide till the last minute because they didn't know what was going to be asked of them till then.

Perhaps in this final section it is briefly necessary to remind ourselves never to say "Now, in conclusion," or "let me summarize," or "as I conclude," or "one more thing and I'm through." All such "terminators" stop listeners from hearing whatever is to be said next. Furthermore, if much is said after such concluding statements, the listeners will say, at least in their minds, "Hey, Buster, you said you were through, promises, promises, promises!" Since all spoiling interventions only invoke disinterest or hostility, it is better never to let the sermon's artful conclusions be obvious.

The Four Persuaders

There are some forms of argument whose precise placement in the sermon is most valuable. Certain forms of logic are hard argument and make final points that are fixed and firm and draw the net on persuasion. Let's turn our attention to these forms and how best to employ them in abetting the argument of the sermon.

The Use of Statistics

The use of statistics to undergird the sermon's argument can be extremely forceful. Caution must be sounded about using too many of these statistics unseparated by comment, however. Statistics crowded one upon another may quickly confuse and prevent hearing. Use them sparingly, a few at a time.

Also, be sure that you always cite the source of statistics, who compiled them, and why they should be regarded as reliable. Above all, be sure with every use of statistics that you keep them tied to the argument of the sermon.

Footnoted Insight

The important thing to be remembered about these persuaders is that it is not generally the insight that adds clout to the argu-

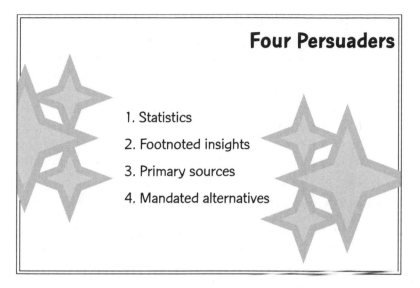

Four Persuaders

1. Statistics
2. Footnoted insights
3. Primary sources
4. Mandated alternatives

ment. When you use a footnoted insight, *what* is being quoted is not nearly as important as *who* is being quoted. So we want to be sure that the source is immediately recognized as someone the bulk of our listeners know and consider qualified to influence our judgment on the matter. The footnotes should be accurate within the source quoted. It is not nearly as persuasive to say, "President Bush once said," as it is to say, "The president said this week in a *Time* magazine interview . . . "

These sources should be cited in the proper research style in the sermon manuscripts or notes. But it should be cited more generally in the oral document. Still, the oral cite should have such authority that the listener knows the material is not yours. The quoted communiqué will then go quite a distance in increasing congregational confidence in the sermon.

Reading Primary Sources

I think it is generally good technique to read directly from a magazine or book, rather than to quote merely words. Reading directly from a primary source should be done if:

1. The portion read is powerfully written and relates to the central argument of the sermon in a key way.

2. The portion read contains long, important segments that would lose something if quoted in lesser ways.
3. Anytime a direct reading from a primary source would appear to add authority and persuasion to the sermon.

Direct reading from current popular books on management or culture will often impress the marketplace mind, especially if people are familiar with the book or its writer. Direct reading has more effect, of course, on highly literate, secular congregations than it might in lower socioeconomic groups.

Drawing Mandated Alternatives

One of the most powerful techniques that can be used in sermons is the careful drawing of mandated alternatives. By this I mean the sermon seeks to draw alternatives, one of which *must* be chosen. This kind of preaching does not always mandate alternatives between good and poor self-image: Either you become committed or you will live in uselessness to God.

The better kind of alternatives draw audiences to the best of two good, positive alternatives: Either you must become committed to community ministry or you must commit yourself to a good life but one that will not leave your world different than you found it. As certain promotional writers have helped us understand, everybody likes win-win alternatives better than win-lose alternatives.

Poetry and Emotive Argument

The old evangelical model for sermon outline—three points and a poem—leaves a lot to be desired, but it does firmly establish one truth: People generally expect or at least don't mind the use of poetry in a sermon. Poetry can be an emotive persuader. If they are read well, even the worst poems can invite feelings of need and a desire for commitment. Which poems to quote and where should they be placed in the body of the sermon? The question of which poems has to do with the taste of the audience.

In a college or seminary chapel, "The Old Violin" would per-

120

haps be less efficacious than something by Keats (perhaps, not). Reading Gerard Manley Hopkins in an inner city mission would not be understood at all. On the other hand, "Mother's Bible" might be. Poetry can be drawn from hymns or the popular songs of the day, from Broadway musicals or classical arias.

The key issue is that poetry should be allowed to adorn or persuade within the sermon. Habitually placing it last will sooner or later be interpreted as saying, "and in conclusion"—and we have already rehearsed the weakness of such pronouncements. But poetry is power. Preachers who have a knack for it should use it freely and with effect.

Walter Brueggemann's Beecher lectures, *Finally Comes the Poet*, are a reminder that we all are open to the emotive artistry and power of sermonic poetry. However, if poetry is "not your thing," avoid it, for ill-used, in insensitive souls, it usually only clouds the argument.

Conclusion

Building a sermon that speaks to and persuades the marketplace mind may be done effectively by observing the issues we have covered. The discipline and artistry of applying these techniques will require that the preacher prepare a sermonic confrontation that is subtle and honors the inductive process. With these things in mind, the sermon will have sparkle, scriptural clout, and an artistic sense of subtle persuasion.

Ten Indispensable Elements of Form and Style 8

The sermon is not a sermon until it is preached, just as football is not a game until it is played. Coaches may plan and rehearse plays, scheme strategies, and exercise the physiques of the players, but football occurs only in the game. Sermons likewise may be planned, outlined, researched, and manuscripted in whole or in part, but they become sermons only on game day. The whistle and kickoff come as the last strains of organ and anthem fade. Sermons that are preached in a congregational context, though, are different from football games in that they may have two starts.

The first start is a congenial beginning that is slightly or entirely unrelated to the text. In this start a bridge is built between speaker and communicants. A bridge is also built between the praise and adoration of worship and the instruction and challenge of the sermon. We have already established that the mode of marketplace preaching is casual. The congenial start has the "nice 'n' easy" feel of casual. We spoke earlier of this easy glide into the sermon's formal start; it may consist of complimenting the choir, thanking the drama team, or speaking of the worship theme for the day.

This congenial beginning is probably also best for preachers who are delivering sermons out of their usual congregational context. Those important sermons delivered to institutional and denominational gatherings will also usually profit from such easy beginnings. Where more formality is in order, preachers will usually comment on and extend greetings to old colleagues, reminisce a bit, and, in general, try a casual and conversational shift into the academic or formal subject matter assigned.

I realize that this two-start sermon is a departure from what most preaching books usually say about the sermon, but ordinarily this congenial beginning should not be dispensed with.

The Empowered Communicator

I call this casual start the speech before the speech in my book *The Empowered Communicator*. Some will object to this informal start because its congeniality breaks the "God feeling" one gets in worship, as solos and anthems settle down upon us to create a receptive mood for the sermon. Some see it as undignified and antiliturgical—in short, as disruptive. There is a sense in which each of these criticisms is true. But particularly in a local congregation, this kind of beginning more often translates as human and warm. For all that it may contribute that is disruptive, it will more than compensate by creating a sense of family and conversation, which, as we have said, is the meaning of the word *homiletics*.

The second start for the sermon is the more formal approach—the offering of the first lines of the written but unread introduction. The audience will say within themselves, "Aha, now . . . down to business!" Still, the casual beginning has served to make the business of the sermon welcome. The moving into this second start will be all the more welcome if the preacher has not confused the casual start with an overdose of "horsing around." The formal approach will capitalize on the first line and a developed attention-grabber. As we begin the formal sermon, the shift from casual to formal should be obvious. The audience should track with the move. If any single word describes the marketplace sermon, it is the word *casual*. Still, at least the thickening of content and the obvious use of illustrations, precepts, statistics, and textual analysis ought to say the main argument of the day is now officially underway.

Once the sermon is underway, there are ten indispensable elements of form and style that will identify and define what the marketplace sermon is. I have arranged these in a decrescendo

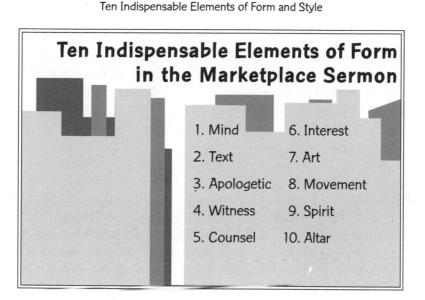

Ten Indispensable Elements of Form in the Marketplace Sermon

1. Mind
2. Text
3. Apologetic
4. Witness
5. Counsel
6. Interest
7. Art
8. Movement
9. Spirit
10. Altar

of values, beginning with those things that should characterize the sermon and that we can control, then moving to those things that gild and build intrigue into the sermon.

For instance, item one—developing a consistently orthodox and steady worldview as defined by who we are—is something everyone can do. So are items two—the issue of the text and its place in the sermon; three—making sure the sermon is a strong defense of Christian truth; four—making sure the sermon bears a witness to the truth; and five—making sure the sermon contemporizes the ancient truth. However, issues like interest, artistry, movement or pace, spiritual power, and altar response are items that not all preachers possess in the same amounts. In other words, every preacher should be able to study and present a content-filled and insightful sermon. The real electricity and passion of communication belong both to the spiritual formation and the desire for pulpit artistry.

In the case of each of these ten elements, I will be referencing each point to a single pulpit scholar who has had more to say about this particular issue than all others. I hesitate in many ways to do this because I am more than confident I shall miss some insight. However, a book like this, and certainly a chapter like this, presumes many limitations. In forming my own philosophy of preaching, I have borrowed so much from these men and women that I want to commend their contributions to your own sermonic form and style as well. Should any of you from whom I have borrowed feel unfairly represented, please inform me and forgive my misunderstanding.

The Mind of the Sermon

The second Helvetic confession says, *"Praedicatio verbi dei est verbum dei."*[1] For discussing form and style, I want to take the character of the preacher as a given, and say that "the preaching of the words of God is the Word of God." This is why Ian Pitt-Watson, for me, writes the fundamental issue of form and style. Older books on preaching have always rooted the sermon's validity in the character of the preacher. If that is invalid, all talk about the rest of homiletics is useless, because the power of this idea is only as strong as the preacher's unwavering commitment to truth. That continual commitment should not change from sermon to sermon.

Sermonizing from week to week will gain a hearing in a congregation only when that congregation believes that the preacher believes something, and they know what it is. In other words, those who listen must be able to locate the preacher's worldview. This means, of course, that the preacher, too, must know what his or her worldview is. I strongly suggest that all preachers write down the various points of their worldviews and, if possible, put next to them a scriptural text or two that supports what they believe. I realize that scripturally documenting all the elements in our worldview may not be universally appealing, but I am convinced most Christians want a preacher who knows what he or she believes.

Pitt-Watson reminds us that it is never possible to know who we are until we know who God is and what he has done.[2] In a sermonic sense, our worldview is inseparably linked to God and our view of him and his involvement in our lives. Who humanity is, our origin and destiny and meaning, are also involved in our worldview. Pitt-Watson declares that the theologically consistent heart of the sermon is the *sine qua non* of biblical preaching. The heart of the sermon should issue week to week from a single, unwavering view of God and humanity. Small wonder, then, that Pitt-Watson declares that the "what" of our preaching is more important than the "how."[3] The "what" is the content of our worldview. This issue of interpretation comes before all others. It comes way before the use of commentaries and word study sources. The sermon is about God before it is about us.[4] Therefore, it is imperative for most that the preacher's worldview remain moored to the text of Scripture. "Theology empowers the ethic," says Pitt-Watson.[5]

A real danger of the marketplace sermon arises at this point. So many of the megachurch pastors have begun seeker services to attract seekers. Theology has been seen as a kind of "white" demon that destroys the secular draw. In tiptoeing around their worldview, an impression might be left that the preacher's real worldview is too offensive to speak about openly. A caution must be sounded. Worldviews are so essential that preachers must not try to give seekers any reinforcement that their own worldview is OK as it is. Nor, God forbid, should they imply their worldview is identical to those who hear their sermon. This soft approach has in every earlier generation fostered unholy syncretisms. Such glitzy appeal distracts the heart with trifles, while the deepest issues of conversion and discipleship go unmet.

Remember that conversion has always been the work of Christ's church. To foster the opinion that conversion is anything *less* than a changing of worldviews is at its heart unethical. It behooves us all to carry into the pulpit a clear understanding of what we believe about God and our world. It should be so powerful that it cannot help but show through. It also is a credit to every preacher of the gospel that all attendees know who he or she is regardless of the state of their own secular stance.

The Text of the Sermon

The second most indispensable element of style and form is the text. I have listed it in second place because, while many would list it as primary, I am always aware that every individual text is

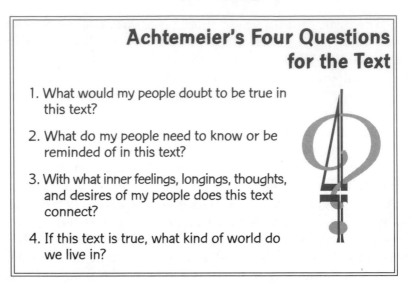

Achtemeier's Four Questions for the Text

1. What would my people doubt to be true in this text?

2. What do my people need to know or be reminded of in this text?

3. With what inner feelings, longings, thoughts, and desires of my people does this text connect?

4. If this text is true, what kind of world do we live in?

interpreted through some preacher's worldview. Never, therefore, does any preaching of the Bible come from total objectivity. The preacher's worldview is a filter determining how the audience will receive the sermon text.

It is difficult not to admire the scholarship of Elizabeth Achtemeier on this subject. Achtemeier has said so many things relative to giving the text its due that I can only condense the contribution that she makes. Her first contribution has to do with making sure that the text is used and fully expanded until all who hear the sermon understand "what God's Word for the church is."[6] She teaches that there are four questions that will delineate and define the text's centrality and sensibility in the sermon.

1. What would my people doubt to be true in this text? Such a question implies barriers that the congregation will have to get over even to give an ear to the text. The question also implies that there is an apologetic function in all strongly biblical preaching. While I want to deal with that in the next section, every sensitive pastor will want to deal with the matter in selecting and clarifying the text.

2. What do my people need to know or be reminded of in this text? This idea will track most closely with what I have suggested in an earlier chapter about selecting the sermon logo. The sermon logo is that ultra-reduced segment of a passage that stands for what the people need to be reminded of.

3. *With what inner feelings, longings, thoughts, and desires of my people does this text connect?* If one adds the word *despair* into this list, it is easy to see that with this question the sermon becomes an existential document. All great preaching deals with existence: its purpose, its meaning, its needs, triumphs, losses, and victories. This question bypasses all study and commentaries; it is largely a question of the soul of the preacher reaching eagerly to the soul of the hearer.

4. *If this text is true, what kind of world do we live in?* The sermon here becomes an ethical device that measures the moral need of the world. Not only does the preacher measure, he or she must diagnose, warn, and rebuke. All of this must be done within the framework of all that God requires of a culture. But the preaching of our message is not just a moral warning or rebuke, it is an attempt to equip others to be the people of God in a wayward generation.[7]

Since the text is the most clearly definable part of what God is saying in the sermon, Achtemeier is most insistent that the message come in terms of the New Testament message. The Old Testament is the language of Israel. Unless we have some connection with Israel, the Old Testament is not "our" book as Christians. Achtemeier spends a forceful part of her argument from the New Testament showing how we are the ingrafted Israel (Rom. 11:17–36), the adopted children (Rom. 8:15–17), and therefore partakers of all of God's covenantal grace. Out of this she calls for the preacher to pair Old Testament passages with New Testament passages in text selection to be sure that we are correctly interpreting God's Word to the new Israel.[8]

I believe that Elizabeth Achtemeier's great contribution to preaching is a clear call to be sure that every sermon derives *from* and speaks *in* a clear way about the Bible. The final steps of preparation of the sermon, before the actual writing begins, is a clearly simplified and memorable outline that can easily be written down or memorized. According to Achtemeier, this brief structure must be scripturally and theologically sound. This will allow the preacher to hang an argument upon it. The various parts of the sermon will not then be too obscure to fit the message. This clearly thought-through outline will serve the preacher by allowing him or her to "bring all of his or her homiletical or rhetorical skills to the shaping of the words and phrases of the sermon manuscript so that it announces that Word of God and enters peoples hearts and minds and wills and, by the inspiration of the Holy Spirit, forms God's purpose in them."[9]

The Apologetic

No two writers better consistently demonstrate that the church must build apologetics into its preachment than Will Willimon and Stanley Hauerwas. We must increasingly be prepared to give the world a reason to believe. The reason for this is simple: "The church exists today as resident alien, an adventurous colony in a society of unbelief."[10] The problem is, as the problem has always been, the society of unbelief is not an exciting but a bland lifestyle. So the liberation of the society will demand that the church speak an energizing word to those who don't believe. How all-important this is! "There was a time when unbelief appeared to be an exciting new possibility, a heroic refusal to participate in the progressive social convention" that the church was.[11] Both Hauerwas and Willimon say that at last the church has some great Good News to proclaim; the success of social godlessness and the failure of political liberalism have made possible the idea that church really is an adventurous journey.[12]

The sermon is an apologetic call to keep the church from staking out its territory and "settling in to guard its turf."[13] Our preaching demands that we take an offensive posture—not a defensive posture. Willimon, in the very title of his *Preaching to Pagans*, suggests that the sermon once again must not only be aggressive in preaching to those outside the faith, but all the church will need to confront it apologetically. Sermons, when they come from a marketplace preacher, exist as a call.

They do not exist just as an aggressive demand but rather as an informative call. We are not just saying "repent and be baptized" (Acts 2:38 NIV). We are really saying, "Here's the information you will need so that you can know how to repent and why you should be baptized." This kind of preaching will not seem unusual in its demand to any in the secular realm. The truth is, in every area of the current establishment, we are used to "schooling" and "seminaring" our way into various community education viewpoints. So the marketplace preacher will find little objection to such pulpit schooling as the sermon must offer so that the potential convert can be brought to an informative stance in every area of evangelism and Christian growth.

Congregationally-specific preaching was once characterized by congregations who were continually catechized and better informed in doctrine. Much of current sermonizing, however, sins in that it takes for granted that everyone still knows all that needs to be known to live the godly life. The apologetic dimension of marketplace preaching starts from a far more basic viewpoint: Don't assume that people know and accept faith or any aspect thereof. Rather, supply convincing argument as to why faith is more reasonable than doubt. Once they believe, supply information that will help them understand how to use the Scriptures in being conformed to the image of God (Rom. 12:2).

The message of the church saves us by doing these two things: First, good preaching will always set us on an adventure that is nothing less than God's glorious purpose for ourselves; and second, marketplace preaching will communally train us to flavor our lives in accordance with what is true rather than what is false.[14]

The Witness of Preaching

Congregationally-specific sermonizing has for its greatest sin the loss of mission. To continually speak to those inside the church as though they were the only ones to be considered important in the hearing of the sermon really only compounds the problem. If Jesus, for instance, is to be considered the model preacher, one must remember that while his sermons speak to those who listen, they are really for the world as a whole. Where local-specific preaching is the diet of the people, there is a bondage to interiorization. There develops an egoistic ecclesiology whose number-one question is, "What am I getting out of church?" Where there is marketplace preaching, the sermon is always reminding the flock that the church doesn't just get together to be told how to live more morally but to remind itself that the church is on a mission.

Thomas G. Long of Princeton Seminary has taken preaching a long way back toward the subject matter of Christ's sermons. His book, *The Witness of Preaching*, doesn't really arrive at a strong sense of evangelism in preaching, but at least it does declare that the church gathers to bear witness that it lives in defense and testimony of all that Christ and the Scriptures call the church to be.

The witness of preaching is most valid when the pastor picks for himself or herself the herald image, says Long.[15] For those who preach, the most important question for the preacher is not, What shall I say in this sermon? but, What do I want to happen? This herald image is borne out in the guiding mark of excellence: Is this sermon good news for me, for us, for them?[16] And the good news reaches a summation in Christ and in the truth that God is in Christ reconciling the world to himself (2 Cor. 5:19).

There is something otherworldly about the notion of marketplace preaching. It is this motif that so often wins it a bad reputation among homileticians. We have made such a god of relevance in preaching that we are prone to forget that in doing this we have actually widened the gap between biblical teaching and current living. The old cliché that "we are so heavenly minded that we are no earthly good" has too much influenced our sermon preparation and delivery. The Bible is in every sense an otherworldly book, but then the message of the kingdom is that, to be relevant, preaching must be future-oriented and touch only on those lasting values of spirituality, meaning, and destiny. Relevance usually does deal with meaning, but so often it does so only in the short run of things. Real meaning lies in mystery, and mystery and relevance are made to appear at variance in much of modern sermonizing.

The church exists to make preaching a call to eternal relevance and to equip its members to make real the gospel of Christ to all who live. This mission will not seem irrelevant when properly preached. On the other hand, the church will have a dynamic reason to be, and the services—once made little by little issues—will grow incendiary and global when the church preaches within its sanctuaries its globally redemptive themes. Such marketplace preaching will give the church an eye that will pierce its poor sanctuary walls and make it rich with vision.

The Counsel of the Sermon

John R. W. Stott quotes P. T. Forsythe as saying: "It is into the Bible world of eternal redemption that the preacher must bring his people."[17] The preacher is inevitably a person who knows that if he or she pleases God and keeps people listening at the same time, he or she must plunge fearlessly into both worlds—ancient and modern, the biblical and the contemporary—and listen to both.[18] John Chrysostom was praised as a man of the world and a man in the world.[19] While no one likes to be called worldly, the relevance of preaching must come from one who knows both the world and God.

But let us not speak too quickly of knowing God and the world as though they are both to be known in the same way. A preacher is to know the world empirically and know God personally. We are to know the world in terms of understanding and to know God in terms of commitment. We should know the world in terms of study and know God in terms of spiritual intimacy.

To know the world in terms of where it is morally and rationally will keep us from appearing naive in the pulpit. But to know it experimentally will mire us in a lifestyle that will allow us no power. John Stott quotes Karl Barth and gives us his insights on how he went about solving this heavy dilemma of bringing the world to the Word and being sure that the meeting is warm with profit for both. Speaking of his dozen or so years in the pulpit, Barth said,

> I sought to find my way between the problem of human life on the one hand and the content of the Bible on the other. As I wanted to speak to the people in the infinite contradiction of their life,

but to speak the no less infinite message of the Bible, which was as much a riddle of life.[20]

Barth went on to describe the dilemma of preaching as a man in the pulpit who lives life in this agony: "Before him lies the Bible full of mystery, and before him are seated his hearers, also full of mystery."[21]

To live and preach in these two worlds will involve both a sense of the adequacy of God and the need of the people. But the people neither know of their need nor the adequacy of God. Since they are so schooled in the things of this world, their whole concept of relevance in the sermon will be not how close it has lived to the world of God but how close it has lived to the media. When Karl Barth was asked years later how he prepared his Sunday sermons, he said it was with the newspaper in one hand and the Bible in the other.[22] Spurgeon also answered this question in a title of one of his *Little Shilling Book* sermons: "The Bible and the Newspaper"![23]

Years ago I heard Martin Marty say in a conference: "Always read the people section of *Time* magazine first, it's the only subject God's interested in." Whether or not this seems narrow to the effective pulpiteer, the truth still remains: Preach only on God and we shall lose both the attendance of God and man, but preach on humanity and everyone will listen.

Nonetheless, this little cliché must not be allowed to dupe us into believing that the Bible is irrelevant. There exists no other burden quite so heavy as that of pulling the biblical Word and the world together. Every preacher who wants to please Christ while wanting to have people listen knows the heaviness of this weekly burden.

Making the ancient world contemporary, however, does not lie, as we might suppose, in addressing everything the national network anchorpersons address. No, the issues of contemporaneity rather group themselves around six questions: What is the purpose of my life? What am I doing here? How did I come to be? Where will I end up? How can I be happy, or happier, at least? What does it mean to be human? Such questions inevitably occupy the attention of every generation.[24]

But how do these questions square with knowing about our world: the world of arts and the entertainments, for instance? It is easily answered. These questions are the big questions at the center of novels and sculpture as well. These questions lie behind almost every story on the evening news and in the columns of the events that compose every newsmagazine. Preach to these themes, and people will listen. Preach to these themes out of the fullness of Scripture, and your congregation will not only listen, it will have answers that are often not found in the arts and entertainment.

The Interest of the Sermon

There is scarcely a preaching book written that does not take seriously the idea of story. Narrative preaching has become a strong claimant for the title of the best sermon style. No preacher has been more vocal or has more to say than Eugene Lowry on this matter. The issue of so many stories in preaching and using a single story as the basis of narrative preaching (and this, by definition, is narrative preaching) has become the model operation of many pulpits in the interest of holding interest.

Nothing quite holds people's attention like stories. The reason for this has to do with compelling intrigue of character and plot. Plot above all locks people in and builds into the sermon a magnetic sense of intrigue. Eugene Lowry defines plot as "the moving suspense of a story from disequilibrium to resolution."[25] Resolution kills interest. It is the opening of the sermon package that keeps people listening, not the laying open of the contents of that package.

Whatever else it may be, plot is mystery concealed. But it is not mystery only, it is the promise of mystery revealed that draws and maintains attention until the mystery is entirely exposed. Obviously, to keep people listening, we must not expose the mystery entirely. The thing is to unravel the exposé, artistically, gradually, and with compelling use of adjectives.

We are, after all, "doing time" in the pulpit, and the time that we "do" is all important. Time is the medium of life, wrote Thomas

Mann.[26] It is within the frame of time that the sermon must serve. If the sermon refuses to take this stewardship of time seriously, then the whole idea of story intrigue is spoiled. None of us like overlong stories. A story must neither hurry nor dawdle. It must work with time, and if it sins against time with brevity or longevity, it loses the power of interest.

One thing is sure, throughout our lives we pay attention to movement rather than still life.[27] Streams are more interesting than ponds. Stories are generally more interesting than precepts. The key thing is that the telling of a pulpit story or the preaching of an entire pulpit narrative sermon should be careful to create the same kind of tension that the original writer or teller of the story felt as he or she created the story in the first place. And what is this tension? This is the tension of remembrance: All great stories do not spring spontaneously from their creators. They grow and develop even as they are told.

Neil Simon once wrote that the "writing of a play is like walking through a dark woods; you are never sure what you are going to meet next."[28] Since stories tell themselves to the novelists and playwrights who write them, they must appear to have the ensnaring interest to the preachers who tell them. When they totally ensnare an audience, they are a force. But to the preacher, the story has appeared with a power of its own and is telling itself. The powerful spell of narration wraps the gospel up in marvelous intrigue even as it unfolds its spellbinding plot.

The Art of the Sermon

Art is, in many senses, the maturing of preaching. I say this because it only becomes art in time. Artistry is not a function we can elect to give a sermon. Art is what we bring to the sermon when we have grown enough as preachers to savor our own maturity in observing life. We are always responsible for making a sermon true and filled with meaningful content. There can be no doubt that narrative somehow develops around the idea of preaching stories. Perceptual preaching takes a great deal longer to garner its art.

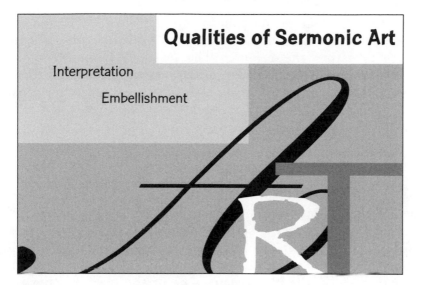

Elizabeth Achtemeier celebrates the God of Annie Dillard, the God who loves pizzazz![29] There is, of course, a great difference between art and pizzazz. Both of them speak of two things: interpretation and embellishment. Calvin Seerveld says in his excellent book *Rainbows for a Fallen World* that all art is allusive. That is to say, all art refers to content beyond that space or form it occupies. Let us, therefore, talk about these two qualities of art within the sermon.

Interpretation

First, interpretation. Paintings, I believe, can be distinguished from art by whether they are only seen or must be apprehended. If one only looks at a Picasso and passes it by, that person has not understood the form and being of art. Why? Because the experience of art has been missed. Art is to be interpreted. This is not to say that it needs to be interpreted by the artist. The beholder is the interpreter. The beholder must decode and record what he or she is seeing. Once this is done, then adjective and assessment must be applied so that one can say for sure that there has been an encounter with art.

The sermon as art means that it is not something to be merely heard. It is something to be listened to, applied, and formally destructured so that its component parts may be tried by the psyche and accepted, rejected, or marked for future use. But the aesthetic parts of the sermon will be not so mechanically applied or destructured. Aesthetically great preaching preaches to the soul and flows from the sensibility of the preacher to the sensibility of the listener. As the preacher experiences art and as he or she ages, the sensibility will grow ever more desirable.

Embellishment

Second, the aesthetics of the artistic sermon undergoes the process of embellishment. Embellishment will be art only as long as it does not smother the precept or obscure the central communicating image of the sermon. The rule here is always excess within control! When the excesses grow wild, the art will be lost. Just as no painter is judged to be an artist because of the amount of paint or the size of the canvas he or she uses, neither is a preacher judged artistic because of the amount of simile or metaphor he or she applies to embellish the sermon. This embellishing process is often lost because, by and large, preachers are not attuned to the world of imagination that feeds this ability to ornament. Preachers too often are not interested in fiction, plays, and poetry. Without a fascination for this great emotive trinity, there will be no real development of aesthetic taste over a lifetime of preaching.

The preacher should never forget that theater and poetry are often created around the same life questions that bring people to church to seek answers. The splendor is that those who work at building an aesthetic spirit are never pedestrian in the way they tell the truth. Where sermons master this love of careful adornment, churches are as packed as theaters.

Elizabeth Achtemeier reminds us that this ability to preach artfully demands a growing use and appreciation of the English language. A lifetime of dull sermons are produced by preachers who live a lifetime without mastering English.[30] Just as an artist can never become an artist without mastering brushes and palettes, so preachers can never become masters without mastering their own tools . . . the words out of which they paragraph their art into the spellbinding genius of their preachment.

The Movement of the Sermon

David Buttrick's *Homiletic* was subtitled *Moves and Structures*. At first, this subtitle seemed like an oxymoron to me. It appeared contradictory. If it moved, it could not be structured; if it is very structured, it will scarcely move. His contribution, however, is well worth considering. The pacing of a sermon has to do with movement and with linking blocks of content together as a freight train would link cars to keep all the issues of the sermon in motion.

Sermons are to involve a kind of sequential talking.[31] This is especially true if the sermon moves according to the classic definition of preaching as conversation. Buttrick includes the following illustration to demonstrate his conversational moves:

> "Are you going to Chicago?"
> "No, I'm going to Traverse City, Michigan."
> "There's a cherry festival there every summer, isn't there?"
> "I don't know, I'm going to a music camp."
> "You're a musician?"
> "Maybe someday—I play the French horn!"
> "Oh, that's supposed to be difficult."
> "I guess so, I'm struggling."
> "Well, take some time to go fishing, there's salmon now in Lake Michigan."[32]

Buttrick deals severely with preaching when it becomes so conversational it can change subjects at this pace. Still, his example does illustrate that incredible speed at which conversations move from subject to subject. As odd as it may sound, it is the casual style that can be used to move the sermon along at an exciting pace. Although Buttrick would deplore using the casual style just to pick up sermonic velocity, the ideas do relate. Hurrying the sermon along may still not supply enough intensity to keep people listening.[33] Neither will merely stepping up the pace of the sermon supply it with power.

Three things pick up the pace but do not hurry the sermon past excellence. First of all, the sermon should have no long illustrations (at least inordinately long).[34] Long illustrations tend to intrigue listeners while they chop the shorter, more effective illustrations from the message. Thus they are discontinuous.

Second, pacing will become ineffective if more than one illustration is used per move.[35] Piling story upon story usually builds deadness, and there is a point at which an overillustrated sermon will not be able to count on the stories to hold attention any longer. It will be like going to a seven-movie marathon at a drive-in theater. There comes a point when the mind will lose interest in the continual stream of narrative.

But third and most important, Buttrick claims that every sermon should move in harmony with a double hermeneutic. Not the Bible/newspaper hermeneutic so often attributed to Barth, but the knowledge of God/knowledge of ourselves hermeneutic.[36] This is the most instructive and substantially paced hermeneutic of all. The key is not only to make a sermon move but to make a sermon move with communication and content.

In the Buttrick concept of moves and structures, the most acceptable mode of outlining is the one-point sermon. Three-point sermons and oral exegesis models will teach more, but they do not cohere as sermons and they lose the oratory in favor of pedagogy. This is to say they begin to succeed at catechism and lose the function of worship and exhortation.

The Spirit and the Life of the Sermon

Donald Coggan makes it clear in his short but glistening work on preaching that to keep our sermons from going dead, there are three integers, all of which must be taken seriously: the preacher, the person in the pew, and the Holy Spirit.[37] Coggan also reminds us that there is no sermon without the Holy Spirit.[38] In the act of preaching, the total church goes into action, since the cast of worship does indeed include these three primary actors.[39] It is deadly for the sermon to call itself a *fait accompli* with only one or two of these integers in place.

The ministry of the Holy Spirit joins with all of the senses in making real worship possible. I would like to recall what I have said in another place: The eye picks up the architecture and worship ornament that are put in place for the preaching service. The senses become the apprehenders of the Spirit. They garner into the matrix of our hearing and feeling the total impact of the spoken word. These senses gatherer the motives of the Spirit for all that he wants to use in terms of sermon impact in our lives.[40]

The Holy Spirit also animates and impassions the sermon.[41] This idea accentuates the fact that passion is not a matter of voice level or the preacher's cathexis with his or her subject. The power of the sermon, its *anima* or life, is a direct result of God's participation in the preaching event.

The Sermon and the Altar

The sermon is not a showpiece of homiletic art. The sermon is there to facilitate God's work of change in the lives of people. All of us are undergoing sanctification. This is to say that God is never finished with his maturing work in our lives. I cannot deny that this tenth element of form comes from my own years of preaching. The altar call has permanently marked my view of what God is about in the world. Therefore, I will likely always miss seeing it in place at the end of every sermon that is worthy of bearing the name *sermon!* Evangelicals have always had the feeling that God wants to do something special in the sanctifying and finishing of each and every one of us. Further, they have assumed that spiritual growth is achieved in a series of leaps of faith that are crystallized leap by leap in specific decisions. These decisions are often made at church and made formally at public altars.

The prominence of altar theology among all evangelicals presumes four things about the sermon.[42] First of all, the sermon is not a speech. The altar, in effect, has every preacher saying, "My words contain his words, and his words are not to be taken lightly. In fact, when his words are through flying at you, you will be given the opportunity to respond to God. This sermon is not all that important, but your response to God is. Think about his words, and focus on your needs. The altar time at the end of this service will give you a chance to bring these two together."

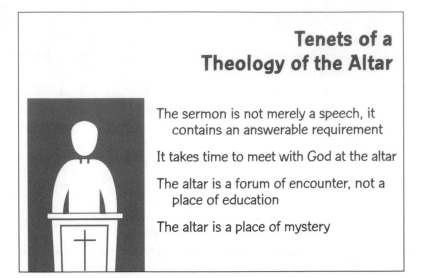

Tenets of a Theology of the Altar

The sermon is not merely a speech, it contains an answerable requirement

It takes time to meet with God at the altar

The altar is a forum of encounter, not a place of education

The altar is a place of mystery

Second, this altar presupposes the issue of time. Time, like every sermon attender, belongs to God. The issue of this sermon is not how long or short it is; the issue of this sermon is that each of us have unfinished transactions with God. The altar will allow you the chance to complete this transaction. How long will all this take? The question is pointless. Will your roast burn if you tarry too long beyond noon? How superficial a question! In the meeting of a King and the receiving of his commission, such questions pale into insignificance. Just focus on your need and his sovereignty. The clock is sent to measure many things, but not this.

Third, the altar is a forum for encounter and not a place of education. The sermon should and does teach, but teaching is not the issue of the altar. The issue is encounter. Experiencing the reality and presence of God is what altars are all about. So do not grieve that your sermon lacked Greek roots or dogma. The sermon sets up the communication channel that brings heaven and earth into oneness so that this necessary and formidable union of heaven and earth may require something of you and you may be filled.

Fourth, the altar is a place of mystery. The sermon should contain the issue of mystery, and house its compelling intrigue. The altar should continue this intrigue as it brings the demands of the sermon to glorious completion. Here, classically, in evangelical worship services, mourners mourned and overcomers celebrated. And in these days when ecclesiology has shifted ever further from seeing the altar as necessary, it is difficult for those of us who have known its counsel to see it abandoned. The altar remains imperative, whether or not it physically exists in the liturgy or whether it is implied. The altar must inhabit and haunt the sermon, as it calls people to a rendezvous with God and encourages them to touch the face of God—decide and be changed.

Conclusion

These ten indispensable aspects of the sermon, it seems to me, are not just enhancers of preaching. They are so fundamental to homiletics that the absence of any one of them prohibits the sermon's coming to be. So let us prepare our preachment out of their confirming wholeness. Let us not presume that sermons that lack wholeness can preach the whole gospel to whole people. These principles contain the *telios*, the completion, without which sermons contain partial and segmented, their work uncertain, their partnership with God questionable.

The Form of the Marketplace Sermon 9

Preparation—how crucial is it? One recent survey indicated that those preachers who take it seriously preach to more people than those who do not. In fact, hundreds more attend those who spend significant time in study than those who spend four hours or less in sermon preparation each week.[1] We should be urged to prepare merely on the basis of preaching better sermons. But, if not, this correlation between study and congregation size should impel us to take our study seriously. The complexity of our calling may here and there keep us so busy that we arrive at Saturday night without a sermon. On those occasions we must quickly prepare to hastily deliver the Word. But such "microwave messages" ought to be only occasional. The "Saturday night special" as a regular fare will not feed the flock nutritionally.

Sermons have historically taken different forms, but those sermons most championed by American evangelicals are expositional. While I do not want to list all the various kinds of expositional forms that preaching may take, this book will argue for the one-point sermon. Title, text, and sermon logo should be picked as we begin our preparation. The preacher should determine in his or her mind what the sermon theme is to be. The single point that the sermon will take will be clearly fixed by considering the sermon logo. In fact, in preparing the sermon, the single point should either determine the logo or the logo the single point. Once that point is fixed, the outline should grow along lines that support the single focus. Illustrations should be chosen to develop the point of the sermon. I realize that for some, the single-point sermon will seem strange. Multiple-point preaching is so extensive among evangelicals that it may seem like a biblical model. I think we would be hard-pressed to prove the method existed among either the Old Testament prophets or among apostolic role models in the New Testament.

Further, one-point communication is the taken-for-granted style of most other public events. It would seem odd to modern listeners if public speakers at community and national media events gave us a three-point outline of what they were going to say. Most great communicators have a single emphasis to communicate—with no alternative subpoints—rarely ending with a poem. A scrutiny of such periodicals as *Vital Speeches of Today* indicates the widespread use of a tightly communicative form grouped around a single, well-developed focus. The older three-point sermon style should be abandoned in this hard-hitting day of single-emphasis communication. This is not to say, however, that the sermon outline might not have several piers that support this single argument. It's just that these points of supporting logic should not be allowed to develop various separate themes. They should all contribute to building a single emphasis, which the sermon develops from the lone theme it champions.

As we move to examine how the single-point sermon is developed, let us again emphasize that there are two kinds of sermon preparation. First of all, let us look at long-term preparation. Long-term preparation will keep sermons fresh and varied throughout the church year and subsequently throughout the course of one's entire ministry in a particular church. If there is no long-term preparation, the preacher may lapse into preaching only on preferred themes again and again. Repetitions of this sort steal the richest, widest context of Bible exposition.

Long-term preaching provides this studied variety by supplying an annual outline on those themes to be developed during the church year. Remember, there really are only about thirty-five Sundays a year that need this varied development. I am assuming that the Sunday morning services receive the lion's share of preparation effort. Once we have been in the ministry long enough to build up a sufficient file of re-usable sermons, the

Sunday evening messages can often come from previously preached sermons. This will mean the "brand new" sermons that require the important preparation can be for Sunday mornings only. If a pastor takes out of his preaching schedule his own vacation times and times committed to special speakers and various kinds of preaching emphases, this will leave only about thirty-five specific sermons to be prepared. Of course, in this I am also including the special religious seasons of the calendar preachers want to emphasize whether or not they are using the lectionary in determining all their long-term preparation. For instance, the Easter season, the Christmas season, Pentecost, All Saints' Day, and Reformation Day may be annually expected sermonic stopovers. After these emphases (for whose recurrent themes a preacher may want to consult the lectionary or other seasonal sources), the pastor may have only about thirty-five special sermons left to prepare. Once a preaching base of long-tenured preaching experience is established, it will be possible for the pastor to write perhaps no more than twenty or twenty-five new sermons a year.

My own long-term agenda was always established by January 1 of any year in question. I took that January 1 deadline very seriously. Within that first week, I would hand our worship leader my sermon titles and outlined texts for the rest of the year. This would give the worship leader a chance to coordinate music and worship with the various approaching preaching themes. This also eliminated the panic that ensues when the preacher and the worship leader reach Friday without knowing what the Sunday sermon is to be. Long-term planning eliminates the crunch of crisis worship preparation.

For pastors who use the lectionary to determine their sermons, themes and outlines will be less of a problem than for pastors who strike out with themes and outlines of their own. While long-term preaching seems to be a threat to many pastors, it is not such fearsome work. With a little practice, it will not be long until most pastors can do this critical long-term preparation at the front end of the year. Such questions as, How often do I want to preach on family situations? Conversionist themes? Deepening the inner life? can be dealt with systematically in December. Then the next fifty-two sermons will touch on the most important areas of congregational and spiritual development. Let us pause at this point and ask about repreaching old sermons and what is required in the art of "warming over."

W. E. Sangster once said that some men think it is dishonoring to God not to prepare a new sermon every time they preach, but the argument in favor of constant new preparation runs thin.[2] Weekly sermons, well prepared, become a kind of gold in repertoire. It is no more true that a great sermon should be preached only once than that a great play or concert should be done only once. The sermon is different than the play or concert in that it is gold always in want of recast and refinement. Great sermons remain alive for years, but they are always open to corrective surgery and new prosthetic logic. As they grow and change and are repreached, they must always be refit to a different congregation. These great old sermons awaiting their next turn in the lectern become one of the finest integers in our long-term preparation schemes.

The second kind of preparation is, of course, short-term preparation. The rest of this chapter will devote itself to what I call the "seven-day sermon." I will outline throughout the rest of this chapter the work of the sermon in terms of the seven days of the week.

Monday's Work: The Text, Title, and Outline of the Sermon

Every Monday should find the preacher settled on these three things: the text, title, and outline of the sermon. The preacher will have determined what text he will use on the given Sunday. He or she will also determine the title and the outline. Again, the long-range preparation, done well ahead of time, may already supply these three ideas. But sometimes the sermon ideas need to be changed, and sometimes during the preaching of long-term preparation there will be a complete revision of what the pastor wishes to say Sunday by Sunday. In such cases, text, title, and outline will at least be completed by the Monday before that ser-

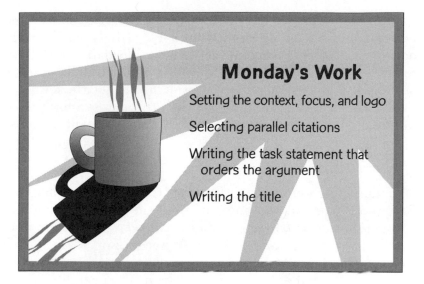

Monday's Work

Setting the context, focus, and logo

Selecting parallel citations

Writing the task statement that orders the argument

Writing the title

mon is to be preached the following Sunday. I honor the contention of Eugene Lowry that in narrative preaching the plot of the narrative sermon supersedes the outline.[3] But even in the totally narrative structure, the plot is a kind of outline. In the company of novelists I have discovered that stories do tell themselves in the process of growing. The narrative of a novel is itself a guiding outline that gradually forms to become the structure on which the story hangs. So should it be for the narrative sermon. There are four specific aspects that I believe will accompany Monday's work.

Setting the Context, Focus, and Logo

On Monday each week, not only is the text and title and outline to be chosen but the pastor should determine the larger context from which the text is to be drawn. Little constructive work can be done until the pastor determines this larger context. Second, the focus of the sermon, which of course will match the theme and title, will have to be chosen. We're talking here about the focal verse, that single verse of the larger passage and context that will serve as the focus verse of the sermon. Finally, from the focal verse the point of the sermon, the logo, will be chosen.

John Henry Jowett genuinely felt that every sermon should be reducible to a one sentence summary.[4] Others object to this notion, saying that if sermons could be reduced to a single sentence, why not print that sentence in the bulletin right after the anthem and shorten the service considerably? Still, the sermonic logo is the beacon that lights the path through sermon preparation and lights the hearers' way on Sunday through the more baroque delivery.

Parallel Citations

Elizabeth Achtemeier rightly judges that Scripture interprets Scripture.[5] Not only can one section of the Bible shed light on another, but using parallel citations will keep the sermon doctrinally correct as it does so. A heresy-free sermon is usually one that safeguards the truth of its proclamation by keeping in constant touch with the Bible. Further, the habit of paralleling will infuse the sermon with a kind of compelling authority. That authority is forfeited if the preacher only relies on the reinforcement of secular illustrations. Non-Bible illustrations may add light to a sermon, but they seldom add authority.

The pastor needs to think through the text using the Bible's center index (and word-study parallel sources). In such study we can arrive at the various Scriptures that might complement or explain the text and focal passage. Again, remember that there is nothing more powerful than letting Scripture speak to Scripture. Wherever possible, let other Bible citations speak to, explain, illuminate, and reinforce both the larger context and the focal passage. This thoughtful development needs also to be done on Monday. For only after this is set firmly in place will the rest of the week's work have the skeletal system it needs to build on.

Task Statement and Argument

I believe that by Monday, the text, outline, title, and the work these are expected to accomplish should be laid out. The preacher needs to define *in writing* the task of the sermon. This written definition is the task statement. The sermon's argument proceeds from the task statement. Notice this will be different than selecting the focus or logo. The sermonic focus and logo is Scripture. This task statement states the single purpose of the sermon. It tells why we are preaching on this subject. It says what we expect this sermon to accomplish. The task statement legitimizes the sermon. It should be written down on the sermon outline, making it easier for the pastor to make his or her way through preparation the next time that same sermon is to be preached. But more than this, it enables the pastor to move through the later stages of preparing. He or she never forgets the exact purpose of the sermon. This purpose may need to be stated two or three times within the body of the sermon. Whatever it takes must be done to be sure that the congregation itself does not leave the church clouded as to why the sermon was preached.

Title

I think, that wherever possible, it is good to arrive at a title early. I know this will be the shakiest proposition of Monday's work. Perhaps a better title will suggest itself later in the week as the sermon's work continues. But on Monday, at least a working title should be agreed upon. This will enable the pastor to do what Ian Pitt-Watson suggests in his excellent book—that the sermon ought to grow within us as a baby grows inside her mother. As we hold Monday's four principles in mind, the sermon can grow orderly within us. This ever-circling outline will gather stuff to itself all week. Whether at our desk or not, we will find gladsome content sticking like Velcro to our growing theme. It will come as serendipity out of life. By Thursday a score of related things will be trying to worm their way into Sunday's child. Of course, you must admit only the most powerful of these ideas to join your emerging communiqué.

Tuesday's Work—Commentary and Word Study

Celebrating the Originality of Monday's Work

In Monday's outline, the preacher will have done his or her own work. He or she will have gone as far as possible in outlining the text. This order allows for the highest possible degree of individuality and creativity in the sermon. Pastors who outline on Monday before checking the commentaries on Tuesday will find people generally commenting on their resourcefulness, creativity, and freshness. Pastors who begin their work by going first to commentaries and word studies will find quite the opposite to be true.

Commentary Work

As to commentary work, commentaries come in many different levels of insight. The pastor needs to keep a varied group of commentaries. It is often good to check a serious and scholarly commentary to get the greatest depth of insight into a passage. On the other end of commentary work should be the simpler kinds of commentaries, such as William Barclay's commentary, strong in its probing, applicability, and straightforward Bible exposition. Between the scholarly and simple commentaries lie the power and practicality of the sermon. The scholarly commentary will give the sermon depth; the simple commentaries will tend to give the sermon application. Generally, it is not important to read more than three or four commentaries on any given passage. This will not take a long time and will usually provide the necessary insights. The problem with exploring more is that commentaries tend to become repetitive after reading only three or four. One cannot escape the feeling that scholars write commentaries by reading them. Thus the whirlpool of commentary insights can be a bit tail-chasing. Time may be better spent in other sources.

Word Studies

The issue of how to get the most out of a Greek or Hebrew text is critical. Word studies can be made too obvious within the body of the sermon, but they can never become too obvious within the pastor's own private study. Word studies illuminate passages with strength and power. Do not hesitate to draw from them what the text is actually saying. Greek and Hebrew word stories often prepackage simple, hurried words as metaphors of power. These classic metaphors will link with contemporary illustrations to freshen and vitalize dull sermons.

Greek and Hebrew word studies do illumine a text, but simple English word studies can do the same thing. I would encourage the preacher never to overlook what can be done through

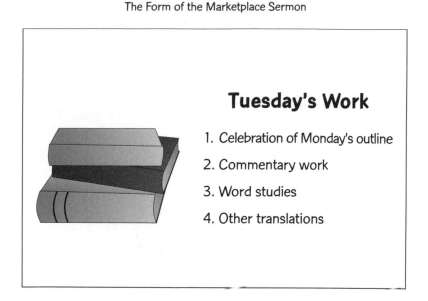

Tuesday's Work

1. Celebration of Monday's outline
2. Commentary work
3. Word studies
4. Other translations

a study of English words. I often find myself bringing to a sermon insights as to the Anglo-Saxon, Norse, or Celtic origin of words that we use in common parlance every day. These supply richness to the sermon. They help people understand where our words or phrases come from. I think this is especially true if one considers such words as *bedlam, Halloween, Valentine's Day,* and *worry.* These words all have special backgrounds that supply a sermon with illustration and interest.

Other Translations

Finally, Tuesday's work will include the checking of other translations. Read varying translations for two reasons. First of all, they widen our understanding of the text. Second, the comparing of translations will give the richest possible synonyms with which to express the ideas of the sermon. By looking at single-person translations such as Phillips, Moffatt, or Peterson, one will come across very personalized individual scholarly translations. These powerful renditions will thrill a congregation for they are often bypassed in the unguided reading life of the parish. Eugene Peterson's new work, *The Message,* is a must. Peterson's grasp of synonyms and the richness of the English language fills the text with light.

Wednesday's Work—Illustrating the Sermon

By Wednesday, the work of illustrating the sermon should begin. Four kinds of illustrations need to be applied to the growing argument of the sermon.

Simile

Never forget that throughout the body of the document it will be helpful for the pastor to liken whatever biblical idea he or she is presenting to something similar to it in everyday life. The words *as* and *like* or *let me illustrate* immediately quicken the conscience of those who listen. With such minimal prompting, they begin to apply the more difficult ideas of Scripture to similar ideas in everyday life. The frequent sprinkling of similes throughout a difficult expositional sermon will make it human and bring it alive to the congregation.

Contemporizing Biblical Ideas

Contemporizing a biblical text or idea may be done in many ways. One of the easy ways is to be sure we are reading the text out of many contemporary translations. In preparation this is especially key. There are some very good kinds of off-the-wall translations such as the *Cotton Patch Version of the Gospel*. I would recommend this one in terms of getting a wholly new insight into the ancient text. Contemporizing Scripture means that, several times during the context of preaching, the preacher needs to say, "This is what Paul's statement would mean today"; "This is how Peter would say this if he were writing his Epistle today"; "This is how the Catholic Epistles would speak to us if they were printed on a folder in our office lounge." In contemporizing the gospel, we are taking the ancient text and putting it in the vernacular of the people. As we said earlier, good preaching is preaching in the Vulgate.

Story

Wednesday's illustrating work will also capitalize on the use of story. On Wednesday it is important to note the story and to footnote the text from which the story is drawn. Every story should come with a footnote. On Wednesday, all that needs to be done on the story is to write down the general theme or title of the story and just enough of the plot to keep it in mind. It can be more fully developed toward the latter part of the week as the preparation continues.

Poetry

I want to argue not just for the use of poetry in preparation but the use of poetic style. C. S. Lewis once said that the language in which we express our faith is not a different language. Still, the tone of this language does range between the ordinary and the poetic. When ordinary language comes into the life of the church, it finds itself under pressure to become a special kind of language to bear its special message. Under this pressure it tends to become either theological or poetical language.

> I think the words "I believe in God" are Ordinary language. If you press us by asking what we mean, we shall probably have to move in one of two directions. We might say "I believe in incorporeal entity, personal in the sense that it can be the subject and object of love, on which all other entities are unilaterally dependent." That is what I call Theological language, though far from a first-class specimen of it. In it we are attempting, so far as is possible, to state religious matter in a form more like that we use for scientific matter.[6]

To demonstrate exactly how this tendency from ordinary to poetic or theological is really worded, Lewis went on to say,

> I begin with three sentences (1) It was very cold (2) There were 13 degrees of frost
>> (3) "Ah, bitter chill it was! The owl, for all his feathers was a-cold;
>> The hare limped trembling through the frozen grass,
>> And silent was the flock in woolly fold:
>> Numb'd were the Beadsman's fingers."
> I should describe the first as Ordinary language, the second as Scientific language, and the third as Poetic language. Of course, there is no question here of different languages in the sense in

155

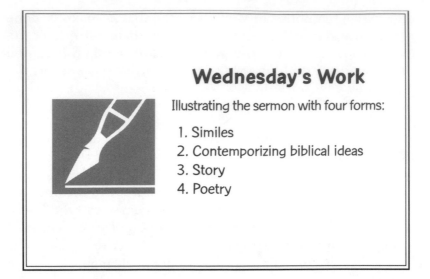

Wednesday's Work

Illustrating the sermon with four forms:

1. Similes
2. Contemporizing biblical ideas
3. Story
4. Poetry

which Latin and Chinese are different languages. Two and three are improved uses of the same language used in one. Scientific and Poetic language are two different artificial perfections of Ordinary: artificial, because they depend on skills; different, because they improve Ordinary in two different directions.[7]

Moving on from the use of poetic language, I would really like to go one step further. As much as possible, we should develop a poetic spirit or lifestyle. Reading poetry, or better yet, studying poetry over a lifetime gives a preacher a firm grip on thousands of insertable lines and phrases that would spice and flavor a sermon wonderfully. If William Blake might serve as a model for this spirit, we might all in time learn

> To see a world in a grain of sand,
> And Heaven in a wild flower,
> Hold infinity in the palm of your hand
> And eternity in an hour.[8]

It all has to do, of course, with our perception—our eye. If our eye is trained to see the world in a particular way we shall pass our kind of sight on to our congregations. To develop this poetic vision is the result of a long-term hunger to understand our world and to define it poetically. Since the Bible is largely poetry, to hunger for this poetic being means that we will enter into a heightened relationship with Scripture itself.

Naturally, therefore, I want to suggest a copious use of poetry in the sermon. I would suggest, that while the poetry should be frequent, it should not generally be dumped in long clippings but offered in short snatches. This will flavor and color the sermon without distraction. There are two kinds of poems that I think translate well in the sermon. Ballads narrate and tell a story. The ballad will generally be welcomed by people, whether it is a contemporary song text, an ancient ethnic poem, or a poem that tells a story familiar to the people. So often, contemporary songs are written in this way and they speak powerfully to people.

A second kind of poem is simply an emotional carrier. Again, I would suggest here that these kinds of poems should be used in much shorter quotes. To use two good lines of Browning or Shakespeare in pithy, life-changing words adds power to the sermon.

Thursday's Work—Crafting the Sermon

To argue for crafting the sermon in a day so bereft of appreciation for sermon artistry may seem pointless. Nourished on how-to homiletics, is there any hope congregations will appreciate or understand? May our sermons always struggle to teach them finer forms of communication! We have become a grade B culture, laments Bruce Lockerbie. We are an entire continent of Philistines:

> Engorged by trivia, yet as culturally malnourished as children fed only on lollipops. For music, we have MTV's rock videos; for art, graffiti and painting by numbers; for sculpture, dashboard icons and lawn statues; for literature, the Harlequin novels; for drama, soap operas and game shows. Our means of discourse has been minimized to depend largely upon grunts and that all-purpose substitute for thought, "Y' know." Our tastes are determined by pollsters and ratings. This week's Top Forty recordings are next week's Golden Oldies. Whereas ancient Greece knew the difference in aesthetics and moral tone between tragedy and comedy, we seem to have lost that power to discriminate.[9]

Nevertheless, the status quo must not dictate sermonic surrender. The sermon must call for aesthetic growth and challenge a junk-fed culture to a better diet. The answer to such a pending reformation lies in the pastor's willingness to craft the sermon.

A Long-term Saturation in Sermonic Artistry

We are not grade B artists. As I earlier argued for long-term preparation in absorbing our poetic world, I would now like to argue for building a long-term saturation in absorbing imagination. The imagination, therefore, must give format to religion and to metaphysics "large ideas tinctured with passion," wrote George Santayana.[10] Don Quixote teaches us, wrote Nabokov, that "reality and illusion are interwoven in the pattern of life."[11] To see this tapestry is to practice our imaginative vision. Such a way of seeing comes by nourishing our imagination with the classics in theater, art, books, and the cinema.

The masters of this vision can teach us their way of seeing as we attend their art. Then their vision will suffuse our own, and our similes and metaphors, having been taught to swim in *their* wide oceans, will swim easily in our own. Our hearers, meanwhile, will grow ever richer. Such schooling in the classics will not teach us how to craft our own sermon. Sermons, like life itself, will seek finer crafting by our acquired hunger for excellence.

"The Runways": Key Stories and Logic of the Sermon

Remember, as we said earlier, that the introduction and conclusion are the runways of the sermon. The liftoff and touchdown are, in flying, the most dangerous times. They are also the times when the sermon is most likely to crash and burn, becoming totally ineffective. However we deal with illustrating the rest of the sermon, the runways must be dealt with carefully. The introduction and conclusion must be written out. This runway crafting will do two things. First of all, it will guarantee the best possibility that everybody will listen and pay attention. It is a general rule that the closer we prepare, the closer people listen. So in the first minute of a sermon it is imperative that we grab the attention of the listeners. If the introduction fails to do this, it is likely that the rest of the sermon will have little luck or will certainly take a long time in getting back our lost attention. Second, one of the major things that carefully crafting the introduction will do is to give the preacher confidence. He or she knows what is going to be said. He or she will say it with confidence because it has been prepared confidently.

Elizabeth Achtemeier contrasts the artistry in the speeches of Jimmy Carter and Winston Churchill. The latter was artistic and his artistry induced his hearers to enter into a new kind of artistic experience. This entering in should describe the whole sermon, but whether or not it does, it must allure the hearers in the beginning and closing moments of the sermon.[12]

If the sermon is perfectly crafted, it will not wander off aimlessly toward an indefinable conclusion. If the conclusion is crafted very carefully, both the preacher and the congregation will realize when the sermon is finished.

By Thursday the preacher should complete the total sermon. The sermon's stories and illustrations should be in place. Statistics and other quoted sources should be entered and all left in readiness.

Polishing the Sermon

Once the initial crafting has been done, the preacher then both on Thursday and the subsequent two days before that sermon is to be preached should edit and polish the sermon phrases. At every juncture and paragraph, the preacher needs to ask, What is the best possible way to make this part of the sermon glisten? He or she needs to ask, Have I chosen the strongest words that most powerfully present the idea in question? The polishing of a sermon can really go on for a long time. Sermons that are to be preached before academic or scholarly gatherings should be prepared months, or at least weeks, in advance. This allows the most careful and meticulous polishing. Someone has well said there is no such thing as good writers, only good editors. In the same way, there are no good preachers, only those who can see things wrong with what will be said. Edit it and then say it well.

It is often a matter of choosing just the right word. Since, as Eric Hoffer once suggested, words "shape thought, stir feelings, and beget action . . . kill, revive, corrupt, and cure," the selection of specific words is all-important in crafting the sermon.[13] In another part of this book, I talk about the task of synonym sifting until just the right word is found. In preparing sermons, I am so dependent on the advice of Humpty Dumpty in Lewis Carroll's *Through the Looking Glass*:

> "When I use a word," Humpty Dumpty said, in rather a scornful tone, "it means just what I choose it to mean—neither more nor less."
>
> "The question is," said Alice, "whether you can make words mean so many different things."
>
> "The question is," said Humpty Dumpty, "which is the master—that's all."[14]

Choosing the word that says it best is a talent learned only in manuscripting a sermon. If this gift ever becomes spontaneous on our feet, it may be because we developed it at the word processor. Words must be made to serve specifically, beautifully, and one at a time.

Pulling of Significant Quotes

Simple, direct categorizings of sermon quotes will be listed according to topic in books like *Stevenson's Quotations*. There are many of these sorts of books available. I generally think that where Bartlett or other quotation sources use long quotations, they may need to be shortened so that they don't divert listeners from the drive and direction the sermon is taking.

Keeping a quotation file of one's own is also a good idea. News commentators, actors, presidents, political figures, people from other nations, ambassadors, novelists, poets—many little quotations can be copied down and quoted directly. Always be careful to cite the source, of course.

The Final Question

One of the bad things about carefully crafting is that it tends to give sermons an elitist tone that may indeed seem offensive or otherworldly to people. The issue is, in crafting the sermon, always trying to think through how the words that we are writing

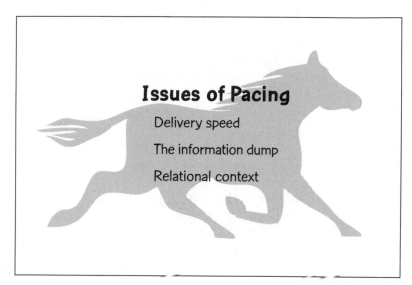

Issues of Pacing

Delivery speed

The information dump

Relational context

down and crafting will sound once they are spoken. Will they sound stilted or phony or overplayed? If so, then the editing work must continue until the sermon's craft fits the service.

A final caveat: Thursday's work is only done when the sermon's conclusion dovetails with the final altar hymn.

Friday's Work—Pacing and Typing

Crescendo Versus Diminuendo

Pacing the sermon is a vital task. Many things are involved in pacing. Crescendo is the general direction in which the logic in the sermon should move for the most part. That is, the sermon should start small and end large in import, logic, and perhaps even volume. As the logic begins to gel, the argument should also come together. The sermon should get bigger in its demand, interest, and captivating power.

This does not always mean that a sermon will end loud in volume. It simply refers to the thing that keeps moving an audience into greater coils of interest as the sermon concludes. Pacing will involve three things.

First of all, the pastor must watch for those kinds of sermons that tend to become tense and remain too tense for people to follow. Remember that tension can be broken by such things as comic relief (the possible telling of a joke) or the using of a light-hearted illustration. A quotation or a read section may break the overbearing, emotional demands. This intentional braking of sermon speed will allow the homily to pick up and begin moving again. Trying to maintain too tight a rope on an audience will generally end in failure.

A second aspect of pacing has to do merely with the amount of material that will be thrown at a congregation within a period of time. It is generally not smart to keep a congregation sitting for a long time while we bury them in tons of information. It is better to save some material for a subsequent sermon in the same series.

A third aspect of pacing is to remember that all the pastor says should be delivered within a relational context. Special speakers can come from outside of a church and deliver highly intense sermons that move at a rapid pace. But, generally speaking, the pastor will be smart to remember that in the local church these people are friends. The pastor will best serve them by giving out information within a relational context, making sure the congregation keeps up with the pace as he or she moves along.

Forte, not Piano

Friday's work must understand that *forte* gives the impression, not just of authority, but of passion in the sermon. However pacing occurs, if it is allowed to move too slowly, then people will lose interest. Pacing can be picked up by an urgent, or at least a more forceful tone of voice. The key issue again is projection. It is such a tendency, once a pastor gets to know the people well, to begin unintentionally dropping the voice in such a way that the drama and the force of the sermon's passion is lost. Simple projection constantly remembered will cause the sermon to come forth as strong and as well projected and therefore important to the hearers.

Transitions

In the sermon, whether in its manuscript form or its outline form, there is but one glue that unifies all: *transition*. Transition is more than mere conjunctions (*and, but,* and so on), but it is conjunctive and without it the sermon lies segmented and unconnected. Conjunctions link sentences. We are talking about connecting the entire sermon into such a tight argument that all separation merges. Howard K. Buerlein suggests the frequent use of "then" and "on the other hand,"[15] to help hearers understand the sermon's argument as it flows from one idea to the next. Transitions guard against stagnation and backwash.

Stagnation is that place where logic and argument stop because the flow somewhere has gotten dammed up behind a stodgy style. What is to be said here? "Transit, my brother and sister." Backwash is that place where logic interrupts itself and the subject is broken by unrelated ideas. The whole sermonic subject starts to fight against the sermon's main thrust.

Interest to Demand

Remember that it is the pastor's responsibility to hold interest. Every sermon moves with three obligations. The first is to tell the truth. The second is to interest. The third and highest goal of the sermon is to inspire. Whatever pacing says, it says first of all that every pastor is accountable for the truth. Truth is the priority of the sermon; this function of the sermon cannot be forgiven, if ignored. But if the pastor or preacher can tell the truth with interest, he or she has reached step two in excellence of preaching. If finally, he or she can tell the truth with interest and manage to inspire and motivate, then of course, this is the highest kind of communication. Just as music may be slow-paced, so also may the logic of the sermon. This will always demand a kind of pacing that never lets the sermon drag.

Saturday's Work—Marking the Moves and Structures

On Saturday, with the outline typed and the manuscripted phraseology now crafted and polished, there are three more steps to achieve. The entire work of Saturday may be done on Saturday morning before the demands of the day begin to wear upon the local pastor. Weddings, funerals, visitations, receptions—these all tend to congest the weekend work of pastors. It is good to arrive at the study early on Saturday, as it is on Sunday, and let Saturday's work be sure that the sermon finds itself being polished in these ways. The important work of Saturday is marking the moves and structures.

Major Structures

In David Buttrick's *Homiletic,* he suggests that structures and moves are the way to be sure that the sermon does not get stodgy or stolid. The first kinds of structures are the major structures of a sermon. Whether or not a sermon has points, it must have major structures, i.e., major blocks of information to be communicated. In a sermon there will be probably between two and four of these major structures. These will gather themselves around the single idea of the sermon. We must be sure as we nominate the structures that we pick the two to four major structures that will characterize the logic of the sermon.

The Minor Structures of the Sermon

The minor structures of the sermon will probably be around fifteen to twenty for a twenty- to twenty-five minute sermon. These minor structures usually take only about a minute apiece. Some of the illustrations or long narrative poems may take three or four minutes. But if a story is taking more than three or four minutes, it is probably outside the boundaries of the one-point sermon and falls into the form that Eugene Lowry calls narrative preaching. Even in narrative preaching there must be points of structure and movement.

By Saturday, the numbers of moves in a sermon should be laid out. In almost all of my sermons preached within the last ten years of my ministry, I had designated the number of moves within that sermon. These moves might be illustrations, quotations, or the like. Most of the structures that moved the sermon along rarely lasted more than a minute or two. The average Westerner now has no more than a three-minute attention span. It is important that the movements, therefore, do not take more time than the average attention span allows. Study carefully all moves and structures to be sure they have movement that does not become too ponderous for contemporary forms.

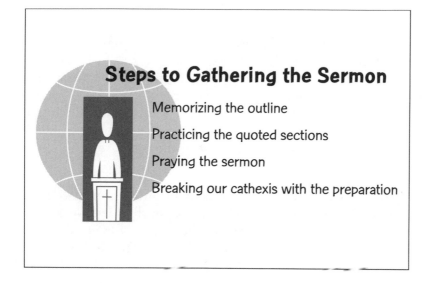

Steps to Gathering the Sermon

Memorizing the outline

Practicing the quoted sections

Praying the sermon

Breaking our cathexis with the preparation

Sunday—One Hour before Preaching the Sermon

The Sunday morning time of gathering the sermon will require at least an hour. Gathering the sermon should be done in four steps.

Memorizing the Outline

The one-point sermon outline should not be complex; the moves and structures should be clearly noted. These sermon notes should also be read through and memorized as much as possible. The more familiar we are with the basic moves and structures of the sermon, the smoother the content and form will flow as we recite it.

Practicing the Quoted Sections of the Sermon

After the crafting is done, some final and particular attention will need to be given to introductions, conclusions, and major stories. Some of these sections may need to be rehearsed to be spoken trippingly on the tongue. To preserve the best phraseology, these note sections should be practiced aloud three or four times before going into the pulpit.

165

Praying the Sermon

As a devotional act before preaching, we may elect to pray through the sermon. Take the sermon, put it before you. Begin praying over its individual points, committing it to the heart of your desire. You will thus gain the energy that comes from trusting God as he enters in and possesses the sermon. Praying the sermon will give it a devotional heart. It will gain for the preacher an authority that is more than that of the scribes.

Breaking

This is the last step on the Sunday morning preparation. It is a step I use to break my cathexis with the study of the week. When I have completed the gathering of the sermon for Sunday morning, I do not continue going over it right up to the time I go out to preach it. I intentionally forget about it for a while. I leave it for a few minutes while I walk out and shake hands with people and greet the guests. By this breaking, I become human. I detach from my "hyperkinetic" connection to my sermon and set myself free. My sermon becomes a human document as I become a human being.

The Delivery of the Sermon

I think there are four factors important in the delivery of the sermon.

1. The demeanor of the preacher. It is very important that all that may be done, particularly for those who are telecasting or in the media, to be sure that clothes fit well, that they hang nicely, that the nicest clothes that can be worn should be worn. It is generally better in the pulpit not to wear sport clothes. The appearance and demeanor of the preacher should in no way conflict or detract from the sermon as the document of power. The new casual mode of our society that has theatergoers dressed in Levi's for Broadway plays has also become the "uniform of the day" in many suburban churches. Here pastors may want to dress down for the sake of identifying with the congregation. Where user-friendly predominates, shirtsleeve sermons can be appropriate, but it is generally better to overdress an audience than to "out-scuzz" it.

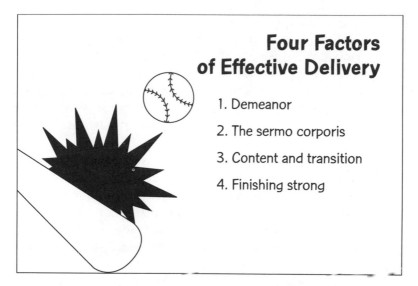

Four Factors of Effective Delivery

1. Demeanor
2. The sermo corporis
3. Content and transition
4. Finishing strong

2. Feeling the force of the truth. Is the Sunday morning sermon work done and in place? Has the pastor lived all week long with the sermon "growing inside"? Then the sermon will be delivered as the preacher feels the force of truth. If indeed we are wound up with our subject, it will become obvious to the people. Great sermons are more caught than taught. Whether the people catch them will depend not just on our appearance and demeanor but on our passion. Does that passion come from a sense of importance we believe is due our subject? Feeling the force of truth will manifest itself in these two things: in the passion with which we deliver it and the body language we use.

Passion is evidenced by emotion and projection. If we are clearly caught up in what we are saying, the hearers will be caught up in it too. Here it is important to feel the force without forcing the feeling. Fred Craddock suggests that the point of the sermon is never to get something off the chest but into the heart. This is to be done not by shouting and pulpit thumping but shouting our whispers. In other words we must be communicators who get across the force of our ideas without getting loud.[16]

It is difficult to have a living subject throbbing in our minds and speech with great passion and remain wooden, stolid, and motionless. We must keep in mind the *sermo corporis*, or the speech of the body. Our day has become a day of the anchor-persons' "talking heads." But talking heads is not to be the mode of the sermon. What we are after here is a subject so vital that it motivates the movement of the entire body, the *sermo corporis*. If our whole body is not demonstrating the force of the sermon, we may have yet to feel the passion of it ourselves. When we feel the passion of it, gesturing will be more than natural. It will be forceful.

3. *Content and transition.* By content and transition, what is meant is that we have at last come to see movement and structure in actual play. Up until this time, the moves and structures of the sermon have all been on paper. But when the sermon is being delivered, movement literally becomes movement and structure becomes structure. From structures, listeners learn orderly, perceptual, and propositional truths. From movement, they receive the energy and dynamism of the sermon's power. The sermon, forcibly practiced out loud, will be sure that there are no "dead spots." There will be no place where logic, story, or movement mires down in a stolid, unconnecting, energy-less delivery.

4. *Finishing strong.* The last part of delivery, of course, means that we should begin and finish strong. To begin and finish strong means that the crafting we did back on Thursday is in place. We prepared a strong beginning and ending. As a result, we do not need to fear that the sermon will lack an ability to draw the net. Keep in mind your stopping place. Stop there and you'll stop strong. Don't be lured by the demon of drama to tack on something full of fireworks you just thought of. Finish clearly, concisely, strong. Avoid the demon of anticlimax. This "drawing" affords the inductive sermon a chance to move listeners to their own conclusions. Remember that neither in the introduction nor the conclusion of the sermon are we trying to tell people what to think. We are supplying them all the information they need to form their own conclusions. If that information is furnished in a proper way with a proper kind of sermonic motivation, the sermon will throb with marketplace vitality.

Afterword

Nurturing a Creative Spirit

Marketplace preaching is infatuated with the word *entrepre-neurial*, which is the way the corporate, industrial world pro-nounces the word *creative*. *Creative* is the way the rest of the world says *artistic*. Artists are interpreters. They take the ordinary and make us see it in ways we never have. Most of us can readily spot and label these entrepreneurs and artists as talented. Seeing them, we often lament our own lack of talent. Talent, we believe, is magic stuff. It's part DNA. It's part luck. It is usually referred to as "it." He's got "it"! She's got "it." If you got "it," you got "it." If you've got "it" flaunt "it."

In preaching, as in any artful endeavor, talent has always been the wrong place to begin looking for creativity. This is true for two reasons. First, *talented people simply do not exist.* Only un-talented people think they do. Talented people rarely consider themselves talented and usually protest the notion that they are. With low self-esteem, talented people often talk themselves out of every claim to special giftedness. Thus a vast army of obviously talented people die feeling untalented. These might-have-beens grow mediocre watching others out-sermonize them. These might-have-beens are surpassed by lesser pulpit talent because of one thing: inferiority. Who knows how many potential Spur-geons, McLarens, and Swindolls have been bought off by their own timid feelings of self-imposed mediocrity? How and why do these non-strugglers surrender to such low self-esteem? Their limited success came to be because they yielded to the great pulpit lie: Creative sermons are superstar stuff, and I am incapable of producing them.

The low self-esteem that fosters this great pulpit lie grows out of the adulation we give to pulpit superstars. Our hyperadmiration of them is an inability to see any hope for ourselves. The resulting self-doubt is not a healthy humility that is spiritually admirable. It is rather a hobbling safety net that keeps us from risking ourselves in the painful struggle to discipline our self-excusing neglect. We often try to copy other people's talent rather than develop our own, so we go on listening to preachers of great reputation and doubt that any of their mega-glory is translatable to our microworld. Oddly, our denials of talent become the very ladder rungs we furnish our heroes to climb past our dull homilies to their own sunny pulpits. Thus, we lock ourselves into the odd ritual of buying their cassettes when we might be selling our own.

A second reason why the issue of talent is the wrong place to begin a discussion of creativity is that *the talented have no way of assessing the level of their talent except by feedback.* As a watercolorist who has galleried with hundreds of others, I have never known another artist who really trusted his or her own appraisal of the work. Until someone else tells them a painting or sculpture was good, they live in doubt, fogged in by inferiority and an inability to measure just how talented they are. Only feedback can teach us the quality of our art. Van Gogh sold only one painting during his life, and in many cases only the appraisal of Theo Van Gogh (his uncelebrated brother) kept him at his work.

In terms of my own writing, I have a sister who is always telling me I have the gift. I love this sister, because she buys my books and even sends them to my other sisters. I have five sisters who have never told me I have the gift. To these I remain only Calvin, a Miller, a brother, a preacher, who might have done better with his life if he had worked at learning the guitar or the piano. Do I have the gift? I cannot say! Others must tell me, or I shall never be sure which of my sisters is right. Feedback owns the day. In the presence of my sister who believes me gifted, I feel gifted. In the presence of the others, I'm unsure. I have worked on this conundrum for twenty-five years now and still have reached only neurotic conclusions. But this much I do know: I dare not start an article on creativity by demanding its link with talent.

In *Spirit, Word, and Story,* I said that not everyone can preach well, but everyone can preach better. So at the outset, let us say that not everyone can be a top talent but everyone can be *more* creative. Four steps are required in developing a more creative sermon style. For those who wish to step up to the challenge, I would like to phrase these steps in terms of nurture rather than achievement. The achievement of talent, like its definition, is impossible to isolate or identify. It washes out like color from new denim. It defies the celebration of our own creativity lest we appear egoistic. Such a celebration is damaging to our art anyway, for once we assume we have arrived, the process of growth stops. Therefore, talent is never a state; it's a pilgrimage. It is a hungering after excellence, an elusive pursuit. It has no finished form. It is never wholehearted in its self-compliment, for what great homily might not be preached better. Even the best of sermons hanker after a second chance.

Accepting Our Uniqueness

While we should never accept ourselves as talented, we must accept ourselves as unique. This is the first and hardest battle of our creative pilgrimage. We throw up every possible barricade to keep from accepting our special status. We are not worthy. We are the nothing-nothings who serve behind the sacred desk. Calvin's theology of worm-hood has "wormed us away" from all homiletical pride. It thus damns us not to humility but to sameness. We cannot see our potential glory because, frankly, we have not even seen our present glory. Preachers should be humble; everyone knows this! For the grace of God to shine through us brightly, we must try to be contemptible in our own eyes. Right? Wrong! Grace means "gift" in Scripture. It is by his gift of grace that we were transformed and called in the first place. That same grace ought to release in us feelings of giftedness and special status. As any good parent, God constantly encourages us to see that we are unique and that our lives contain some once-in-a-universe gifts that must be given to the world or the world will be poorer.

I recently passed a sharply dressed lad of seven years in the hallway of the church where I serve as interim pastor. I lowered my six-foot frame to one knee, coming to his height. He smiled warmly at me, "I like your sermons," he grinned.

"Really," I probed, "whatever for?"

"Because you're funny . . . you're a good preacher."

There was no hint of flattery in his young, bright eyes.

I felt flattered. Yet we all bask in and are healed by the compliments of children. Thinking of how seminary enrollments are thinning and fearful of what they might become in the future, I encouraged him, "Maybe you'll preach when you grow up."

"Not me," he beamed, "I'm an actor!"

"You're going to be an actor?"

"Nope . . . already am! I do television commercials and speaking parts in community theater."

I enthusiastically hugged him. I was glad he hugged back, because I felt audacious hugging a real actor who knew it; it was like hugging a Redford or a Willis in process—our insecurity always needs permission to hug these who are very sure of themselves. What glorious parents this boy must have to give him such self-certainty.

There are three ways we gain such self-certainty, and they all have to do with living out our role in our faith community. First, we must have faith in our community. Our community will from time to time affirm our talent by compliment. Let us trust our community's appraisal at such moments. Let's use their compliment as a springboard to take that leap of faith into strong self-image.

The second and harder mode of affirming our uniqueness will be found in overcoming the negatives of our feedback community. Every church offers a terrible double bind to its leadership. In seasons of celebration and joy, churches make preachers feel unique. In seasons of criticism and pain, they make preachers feel rejected and worthless. Still, negative feedback offers us the

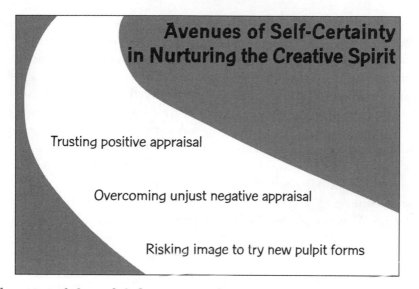

Avenues of Self-Certainty in Nurturing the Creative Spirit

Trusting positive appraisal

Overcoming unjust negative appraisal

Risking image to try new pulpit forms

best possibility of defining ourselves. Criticisms are the physicians of our art. We should bless their diagnosis and proceed with the sermonic surgery they prescribe.

As to real pulpit creativity, only one fearful trial can tell us the level of our talent: Risk! This third component of nurturing our creative spirit has to do with our willingness to take chances with our ego in full view of our community. To discover if our suspected talent really exists, we have to put it on display! But behaving creatively in front of those we love paralyzes us with fear. Peer-fear is a pulpit demon. He is a leering exhibitionist. His fiendish laughter mocks us into sameness. Finally, we are so afraid of him we champion a killing Sunday. Normally we bury our great ideas in three points and a poem: It goes better with the anthem.

How did this peer-fear first get started? It began in the third-grade pageant where we spoke too quietly to be heard and twisted our shirttails in our fists. We looked at the floor and turned sideways to the audience. Now its strongest manifestation is passionless preaching. But make no mistake, it's the same grade school fear of embarrassing ourselves in front of our community. Now it causes us to drop the force we need to sell our oratory.

The risk of creative exposure is frightening. It spawns those "going public" stomach knots and Pepto Bismol neuroses. Closing our sermon by singing a song may or may not work. Mono-loguing Hosea instead of preaching it may or may not work. Oral interpretation of a Vachel Lindsay piece; playing the piano as a part of the sermon; introducing a combo in which you have a part; inviting a fellow staffer in to help you preach a sermon for two—none of these things may work. But the risk of new agenda is prece-dent to all discovery . . . *all!* The risk may tell us we have no tal-ent or it may open a glorious, new way of seeing ourselves. Risk is fearful. But it is the most definite step to defining ourselves.

To keep at bay the fear of being embarrassed in a big way, it is sometimes good to try any new pulpit form first in another congre-gation. This is exactly a Broadway producer's reason for opening a play off Broadway. The reviews come out a comfortable distance from the risky place he really wants to make the performance work.

Barbara, my wife, and I often do pulpit readings together. We did not try this at our home church first. Some years ago we were going to Toronto to lead a couples conference and I suggested that some of the dramatic pieces I was reading would work very well with two readers. "Look," I said, "why don't we try this in Canada. We're a whole nation away from where we really have to succeed. If it works there, we'll take our act back to our local pulpit. If it bombs, we'll return to our church unscathed by the bad reviews of critical Canadians." It worked beautifully, and we took it back with us.

But most times the discovery of any new suspected area of cre-ativity will have to be tried at home. Confidence will come only as we take the risk and measure the feedback. It is really the whole process in reverse. Because it worked at home, we can export it to other gatherings. These distant audiences then can serve as in-valuable reviewers of the new form. Those furthest from the parish will give us a more frank, honest-to-goodness-body-language appraisal.

Observation and Imitation

Let's leave the creative spirit for a moment and turn to creative application. The creative spirit says, I want to be . . . no, I'm starved to be more creative in my preaching. But creative application is the result of a leap of faith that stops brooding "I wish I were" and cries "Geronimo!"

The Sensate Dynamic

Only two basic dynamics determine pulpit creativity. The first is the *sensate dynamic*. Noncreative preaching (indeed, noncreative anything) relies almost entirely on our thinking faculty ("left-braining" your way to pulpit acceptance). But creative preaching depends upon the feeling or sensual faculty. We who must continually give out the substance of our souls must be continually gathering something into our souls as well. The problem is that preachers are so bound by the logical hunger (how is this Scripture to be explained?) that they give little time to the sensual world (how is this Scripture to be *felt?*). This latter question is the primary question for the creative person.

The sensate must inhabit the rational. The best communicators are indeed those who impregnate their communiqué with sensations that must be picked up by the nervous system as well as the gray matter. No wonder Flannery O'Connor wrote:

> The beginning of human knowledge is through the senses . . . where human perception begins . . . you cannot appeal to the senses with abstractions. . . . The first and most obvious characteristic of fiction is that it deals with reality through what can be seen, heard, smelt, tasted, and touched.[1]

Until we communicate sensually, we will, for most, have only a ponderous and boring speech. C. S. Lewis long ago said that it was a mistake to think that our experiences are concrete and can be communicated as "concrete experiences" with precise and literal language. Emotion spoils that concreteness, but this is the glory of emotion.[2] It opens us up to a level of rapport that only emotion can establish.

Basically, emotion is the stuff of religion. In his novel *Job: A Comedy of Justice*, Robert A. Heinlein said that religion was the most powerful drive in the human spirit, and when it was present you could "smell" it. It is pointless to say that great preach-

**Four Forms of
Sensate Encounter**

Live art forms

Audio art forms

Video art forms

Joining an artistic community

ing is mainly teaching the Scripture. Great preaching is making the audience feel the Scripture: It is a sensate immersion in such things as the fall, the flood, the cross.

But more than speaking the emotion of the soul, the sermon awakens the emotion of hunger. This is a fourth-dimensional hunger—a terrible craving for the world of the spirit. This is a liminal hunger (remember the word *liminal* comes from the Latin *limen* for "threshold") for the unseen world of spiritual reality. This unseen world begins a sensate encounter. It must be touched, felt, and seen.

Bruce Lockerbie elicits the German idea of *Sehnsucht* as that elusive drive at the heart of the church's communication. In a sense, our best word for it is *homesickness,* that longing for union with Christ that thrills us with future hope. It is time to cut up your acetate slides and academic word studies. We need to touch this glorious *Sehnsucht.* Throw away your crutches when you talk to us of heaven. Make us see that city. Let us feel the high clear air of his transcendence. C. S. Lewis referred to this homesickness as "our inconsolable secret . . . our lifelong nostalgia, our longing to be reunited with something in the universe from which we now feel cut-off."[3]

The rational now must bow to the liminal, and the language

of feeling must have the day. Madeleine L'Engle wrote long ago of Christmas:

> This is the irrational season
> When love blooms bright and wild
> Had Mary been filled with reason
> There'd have been no room for the child.[4]

The sensate must replace the rational.

The sensate may be encountered in four areas. First, we must apprehend it and try to appreciate it. It is the hunger of great writers and thus the substance of great books to sense true reality. This reach to feel inhabits the world of reading as a whole. I recommend an indulgence in fiction—good fiction (classics are best)—to study how good writers make us emote. I do not argue for fiction alone; I have found myself weeping during the reading of Harrison Salisbury's *900 Days at Leningrad*, or Dee Brown's *Bury My Heart at Wounded Knee*. I found myself enraged when I read Malcolm Muggeridge's *Sentenced to Life*, awed when I read Barbara Tuchman's *A Distant Mirror*, and laughing out loud when I read James Herriot's *All Things Bright and Beautiful*. But plays, too, are contrived to make whole theaters emote. Their creativity is marvelously transcendent. We move through several fields of emotion in many works. I laughed, I cried, I became enraged, and I was awed at my first reading of *Cyrano de Bergerac* and the *Merchant of Venice*. In *Bech is Back*, John Updike's account of a Holy Land tour caused me to laugh so hard that my wife had to restrain me. Reading is a primary way to garner a sensate pulpit mystique.

Hearing is a second way to develop this sensate pulpit dynamic. Many great books and plays are recorded on cassette. These so abound in bookstores that even the busiest of pastors are furnished little excuse for failing to encounter the sensual side of creativity. Novels, sermons, and great philosophies are as accessible as the gaping slot of your tape player. For those who are prone to gorge their mind only with pop gospel tapes, for shame! Get out of the easy listening mode and into a critical listening mode.

Third, watching is the "hot" medium. "Video-ing" your way into the best of cinema is here. But beware, watching is addictive and can make you a video-holic, couch-lounging, pulpit-potato. So determine that your watching will be measured.

Fourth, you can make your watching live by joining a community playhouse or any theater series where there is live drama. Actors before the curtain and preachers before the sermon have many things in common—the cold death sweat in the palms of the hands, the agonizing fear that an incipient Alzheimer's will storm through our souls midsermon and leave our minds vacant. Actors and preachers also are alike in that both depend upon the audience for performance feedback. But in one way, preaching remains quite different than a play. Preaching is a performance done once; it comes live and cannot be edited or retracted, even in part. What you see is what you get. Talk about the sensate dynamic! While we try to speak of Christ or the glory of the cross, we suddenly must switch to track two of our minds. Preaching must deal with feedback midperformance. Is our message overdone (hammy), underdone (cool), or unseasoned (bland)? But our suffering knows an intermittent glory! On every seventh Sunday things click. The babies don't cry. The children watch. The hardened golfers are rained out. The old people turn their hearing aids up and lean forward in their pews. The angels sing. And we bring the greatest exposition of all time. Our gestures are seismic, our text crackles with fire, and our psyche congratulates us in the splendor of our calling. "Great Scott! We're preachers!"

Feeling as Suffering

Still one further question demands examination: Can preachers authentically preach with emotion of things that have not stirred or shaken their own existence? How important is bleeding to those who want to speak to the bloody? Does not suffering fill a mighty sermon with a sensitivity unavailable to the little talks of those preachers whose lives have known only minor pain?

There does seem to be more than a casual connection between Toulouse-Lautrec's art and his deformity. Demosthenes stuttered his painful way to enthralling oratory. Byron hobbled through his fleet verse on a club foot. Besides the physical challenges that sensualize art, there are countless examples of those who climb psychological barriers to sensate enthrallment. Bach was considered heretical for using his thumb on the keyboard. Shakespeare's popularity caused many to say his work was trivial![5] Pain itself does not make us preach well, but it builds a sensitivity that does make our particular emotional experience speak to that of the whole. Only weathered wood makes singing violins.

As potential creators, we ought to say, "What is here that might instruct my own creative yen? How can I employ this pain or use that hurt?" If nothing else the pain will tenderize the preacher and the preaching, like water flowing from a fountain gathers sunlight in the process of fall and splash.

The Imitation Dynamic

The imitation dynamic asks only two questions: Am I impressed by this, and can I do it too? The first question is again a critical question and the second is a question of risk. It is this "Can I do that?" question to which we must turn. But before we do, we need to ask, "Is imitation fair or is it plagiaristic?" We all learn by imitating. Children learn almost everything this way—all sensate aspects of our appreciation are learned by imitation. Further, they are learned in community. As we gather together to hear and watch each other, we instruct each other. Artists watch each other paint; writers read each other's writing; and preachers (lamentably ofttimes) preach each other's sermons. But before we imitate, let us add to what we see and hear with the uniqueness of our own form. Then the imitation of others can become a synergism made authentic by the addition of our *own* style and substance. There is much truth in the old cliché: Copy from a single source and you're a plagiarist; copy from two or more and you're a creative writer.

Remember, Shakespeare did not invent *Romeo and Juliet*, he only deleted and accreted his own rendering of an Italian source (this is true for most of his plays). Neither did Leonard Bernstein totally invent *West Side Story*, he merely deleted and accreted *Romeo and Juliet*. The key thing is that each person in turn was highly creative and a genius in his splendid imitation.

The final question in this section is the question: "Can I do this?" One of my favorite songs from A *Chorus Line* is "I Can Do That"! The song is the testimony of a young person who, in seeing another entertainer get rich while he dawdled along with another art, said to himself and to his own credit, "I can do that." Nurturing the creative spirit means that along the dawdling course of our uncreative lives we say out loud—loud enough for God and the entire world to hear it—"I can do that!"

Jesus: The Best Watching Point

Before we can honestly say, "I can do that," we must ask who the preacher's best role model is. The obvious answer is Jesus. In studying how Jesus preached (for all but the totally impious), the statement "I can do that" will come slowly. Watching Jesus will lead us to the conclusion that it is not only the "what" of preaching that is important but the "how." Aristotle laid down the importance of crafting the sermon when he said, "It is not enough to know *what we ought to say*: we must also *say it as we ought!*"[6] Bruce Lockerbie reminds us that Jesus' sermons came with simplicity and directness of style. They had originality and integrity. His parables are sensate and most pictorial and yet never overwritten or extravagant. He never stumbled over clichés or resorted to melodrama.[7]

Watching Christ, we gain the sensation of sermon as thrift. One wonders how Christ's marvelous sermonic economy could ever prompt the verbose and redundant pulpiteers it seems to sire in our times. A closer imitation of Christ's economic style may also shorten the sermon into listenability!

Once we decide to run the creative risk of trying some new form, the danger arrives. Sometimes we find that we really *could not do it*. But we have not failed! We have only better defined ourselves by locating one creative form that is not to be ours. Still, in the attempt, we nurture our creative spirit. Learning the limits of our creativity is also important. The money on the game is that our listeners also see and learn our creative limits. But, never mind, from time to time they also see our joyous successes. Actors are never remembered for the shows that close off Broadway. They are enshrined only for those standing-room-only nights,

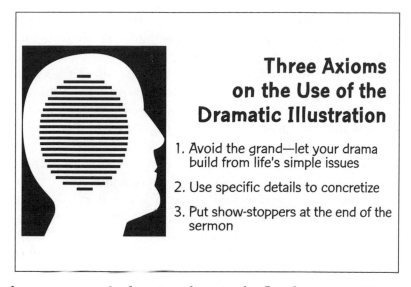

**Three Axioms
on the Use of the
Dramatic Illustration**

1. Avoid the grand—let your drama build from life's simple issues

2. Use specific details to concretize

3. Put show-stoppers at the end of the sermon

when roses smashed against them in the floral stonings. We, too, will also be best remembered for the times we did it well.

Drama and Humor

Drama and humor taken together label us as creative. Their absence labels us as BORRRRING! "Dramatic" is that tenuous quality of the sermon that falls between those two deadly prefixes of "melo" and "un." Evangelists have had a long-standing reputation for sermon illustrations that stay too close to these poles. Finding an authentic way to illustrate a sermon that finds a comfortable middle ground for drama is most important. Here are three important considerations for those who find this medium cool enough to handle.

First, let your drama build from the simple issues of life. Jesus' parables thrived with the power of simple dramas. Annie Dillard won a Pulitzer Prize by describing such things as a mockingbird swooping downward from a roof gutter. Her description is powerful and dramatic. Barbara Tuchmann won a Pulitzer Prize for describing such things as the lusty singing of a confident German army. Both are beautiful in context. But in the pulpit it is better to side with Annie Dillard than Barbara Tuchmann. To build contagious attention out of simple drama is better than to risk your-self with Cecil B. DeMille illustrations that so easily smuggle us to the "melo" and "un" poles.

The second rule of illustrating says that specific details give il-lustrations reality. Powerful illustrators harness the emotional storms with the cables of time, date, and place. History and the-ology abound with powerful tales that can move an audience to tears, but such dramas are powerful precisely because they come furnished with specific information. A lack of specific handling allows the power to float away in the direction of clouded fiction. The supplying of specifics will say to all its auditors, "Listen to me—I am as true as the Bible I am being used to illustrate!"

A third rule is that an especially powerful illustration tends to be a showstopper and should therefore be placed at the end of the sermon where the show can come to a logical end. At the ser-mon's end there is nothing left over that could be considered ei-ther "melo" or "un" dramatic or even anticlimactic. The only cau-tion that needs to be sounded then is: Does this dramatic illustration end the sermon leaving people wanting to serve the call of the sermon?

A case in point: I well remember an evangelist who told a heartrending story about a little boy at a church prayer meeting who requested prayer for his abusive father to be "saved." Ac-cording to this raconteur-evangelist, the boy's father learned that his son had requested prayer for him publicly. "If you ever ask that church to pray for me again, I'll beat you to death," said the unrepentant father. The boy, ignoring his father's threat, did re-quest prayer once again for his father. True to his word, his abu-sive father, livid with rage, took a tire iron (or maybe a pipe wrench, I can't recall) and beat his small son senseless. The il-lustration closed the sermon as violently as Rambo had once dis-patched the Vietcong. As we, the benumbed, stood to sing the invitation, the children were in tears. Many of them came for-ward ostensibly to confess Christ but really they were only feel-ing sorry about the poor little boy who "died lying face down in a pool of blood" at the sermon's end. My own four-year-old daugh-ter said to me on the way home from church, "Dad, it sure was too bad about that little boy lying face down in a pool of blood, wasn't it?" I was horrified that her little mind had been traumatized by a drama that was abusive and destructive. Drama should serve, not sever, the human spirit.

Jokes, per se, are best avoided. They can serve our creative reputation, but even when they are done well, they lend a note of contradiction to the overall seriousness of what a sermon should be about. Using stories that deal lightly with light interest is another matter, however. Life has its funny moments, and to preach life means that by necessity the sermon will, from time to time, be funny. If such welcome and wholly acceptable humor finds its way into preaching, the clever use of adjectives may be the way it is done. Description more than event usually supplies the humor.

One further observation: Leisure and lightness keep the same company. Humor works best where the sermon is unhurried in its delivery. If its speed is hyped with a heavy sermonic agenda (like evangelism or fund-raising), the pace can cancel the lightness. The vocal pause and the planned pace invite laughter. Not that laughter is good for the sermon, but please let it be remembered that laughing and crying (emoting in general) bring congregational separateness into unity. When people emote together, they come together.

Conclusion: Crafting Life Feedback

The creative spirit is always a critical spirit; it appraises all incoming data, especially sermon response. As people give us feedback, we interpret. As we interpret, we edit. The creative process is always one of editing. Once we become critical thinkers, we will find ourselves asking in the middle of novels, plays, movies, concerts: How could these bad spots have been eliminated and the good spots elongated? The surest evidence that our creative spirit is maturing is this critical spirit. All artists are artists because they have this spirit. Naiveté is the only other option. Those who cannot edit the creative feedback will prematurely celebrate poor art. Such a mature spirit comes only with wide taste and experience. It is only those who have listened critically to a great number of sermons who begin to judge the quality of all sermons.

The creative spirit is nurtured by time and evaluation. Evaluation of any art form, including sermonic art, is enhanced in its clout as time passes. Long-term preparation is the best guarantee of the best scrutiny. Putting a sermon away for a rest and taking it out after long periods of time will allow the most mature judgment to be made about its real quality. Those special sermons that bear great importance in the life of a church should be given this refining edge of long-term preparation.

But whatever our mode of editing, we must remember that without it, creativity never grows and matures. The creative spirit is nurtured by those who care about excellence, and excellence is never merely a matter of inspiration. Rather, it is a matter of working through our suspected artistry into a more certain glory. When all of this is in place, we will understand how inspiration must reckon with our best judgment. *Art* will then become a real word for us, and our suspicions that we have talent will grow.

Notes

Preface

1. Joseph Seaborn Jr., *Celebration of Ministry* (Grand Rapids: Baker, 1990), 31.

2. Sir James Frazer as quoted by Harold Kushner in *Who Needs God* (New York: Summit Books, 1989), 148.

3. Jerry Bridges, *The Practice of Godliness* (Colorado Springs: NavPress, 1983), 57.

4. Thomas Watson as quoted by Donald S. Whitney in *Spiritual Disciplines for the Christian Life* (Colorado Springs: NavPress, 1991), 53.

5. Kenneth S. Kantzer, "What Happens When Koreans Pray," in *Christianity Today*, August 16, 1993, 13.

6. Henri J. M. Nouwen, *Reaching Out: The Three Movements of the Spiritual Life* (Garden City: Doubleday and Co., 1975), 30.

7. David Swartz, *Embracing God* (Eugene, Oreg.: Harvest House Publishers, 1994), 117.

8. Eugene H. Peterson, *The Message* (Colorado Springs: NavPress, 1993), 21.

Chapter 1: Back to the Marketplace

1. Charles Haddon Spurgeon as cited by James D. Berkley in *Preaching to Convince* (Waco: Word, 1986), 13.

2. George Bernanos, *The Diary of a Country Priest* (New York: Macmillan Paperbacks, 1937), 30. As cited by James W. Kennedy, *Minister's Shoptalk* (New York: Harper and Row, 1965), 34.

3. Walter Brueggemann, *Finally Comes the Poet* (Minneapolis: Fortress, 1989), 43.

4. Tom Long, *The Witness of Preaching* (Louisville: Westminster Press, 1989).

5. Tim Timmons, "Why Should They Listen to Me?" from *Preaching to Convince*, ed. James D. Berkley (Waco: Word, 1986), 20.

6. James D. Berkley, ed., *Preaching to Convince* (Waco: Word, 1986), 41.

7. Nan Kilkeary, *The Good Communicator* (Evanston: Quikread Press, 1987), 10.

8. Ian Pitt-Watson, *A Primer for Preachers* (Grand Rapids: Baker, 1986), 23.

9. A. J. Conyers, *The Eclipse of Heaven* (Downers Grove: InterVarsity Press, 1992), 96.

10. Conyers, *The Eclipse of Heaven*, 91.

Chapter 2: The Audio-Video Sermon

1. Donald Coggan, *Preaching the Sacrament of the Word* (New York: Crossroad Publishing, 1987), 65–66.

2. Merrill Abbey, *Communication in Pulpit and Parish* (Philadelphia: Westminster Press, 1973), 123.

3. Charles L. Bartow, *The Preaching Moment* (Nashville: Abingdon, 1980), 62–63.

4. Thor Hall, *The Future Shape of Preaching* (Philadelphia: Fortress Press, 1971), 34.

5. F. Dean Lueking, *The Art of Connecting God and People* (Waco: Word, 1985), 58.

6. Neil Postman, *Amusing Ourselves to Death* (New York: Viking, Penguin, 1985), 79.

7. John P. Newport, *Life's Ultimate Questions* (Dallas: Word Books, 1989), 95.

8. Peter Marshall, *Mr. Jones, Meet the Master* (New York: Fleming H. Revell, 1950), 31.

9. Pitt-Watson, *A Primer for Preachers*, 37–38.

Chapter 3: TelePrompTing the Text

1. David Buttrick, *Homiletic* (Philadelphia: Fortress Press, 1987), 239.

2. Richard Baxter, *The Reformed Pastor* (Portland: Multnomah, 1982), 19.

Chapter 5: Packaging Preaching: Worship in the Marketplace

1. John Claypool, *The Preaching Event* (Waco: Word, 1980), 87–88.

2. John A. Broadus, revised by Jesse Burton Weatherspoon, *On The Preparation and Delivery of Sermons* (New York: Harper and Row, 1944), 335.

3. David H. C. Read, *Preaching about the Real Need of a Real People* (Philadelphia: Westminster Press, 1988), 72.

4. A. J. Conyers, *The Dimming of Heaven* (Downers Grove: InterVarsity Press, 1992), 11–12.

5. Fred Craddock, *Overhearing the Gospel* (Nashville: Abingdon, 1978), 16.

6. John Killenger, *The Centrality of Preaching in the Total Task of Ministry* (Waco: Word, 1969), 46.

7. Gerald Kennedy, *The Preacher and the New English Bible* (New York: Oxford University Press, 1972), 7.

Chapter 7: Crafting the Marketplace Sermon

1. Elizabeth Achtemeier, *Preaching from the Old Testament* (Philadelphia: Westminster-John Knox Press, 1989), 110.

2. Thomas G. Long, *The Senses of Preaching* (Philadelphia: John Knox Press, 1946), 60.

3. Ronald J. Allen, *Preaching for Growth* (St. Louis: C.B.P. Press, 1988), 22.

4. Achtemeier, *Preaching from the Old Testament*, 17.

5. James Black, *The Mystery of Preaching* (Grand Rapids: Zondervan, 1978), 80.

6. Harold T. Bryson and James C. Taylor, *Building Sermons to Meet People's Needs* (Nashville: Broadman, 1980), 70.

7. Robert McNeil, *Wordstruck* (New York: Viking, 1989), 3, 27.

8. Calvin Miller, *Spirit, Word, and Story* (Dallas: Word Books, 1989), 110.

9. Bruce Salmon, *Storytelling in Preaching* (Nashville: Broadman Press, 1988), 40.

10. Clyde Fant, *Preaching for Today* (New York: Harper and Row, 1975), 99.

11. H. Grady Davis, *Design for Preaching* (Philadelphia: Fortress Press, 1958), 115.

12. Eugene Lowry, *The Homiletical Plot* (Nashville: Abingdon, 1985), 23.

13. Ralph G. Turnbull, *The Preacher's Heritage Task and Resources* (Grand Rapids: Baker, 1968), 129.

Chapter 8: Ten Indispensable Elements of Form and Style

1. Pitt-Watson, *A Primer for Preachers*, 14.

2. Ibid., 21.

3. Ibid., 23.

4. Ibid., 21.

5. Ibid., 22.

6. Achtemeier, *Preaching from the Old Testament*, 54.

7. Ibid., 54–55.

8. Ibid., 56–57.

9. Ibid., 60.

10. Stanley Hauerwas and William H. Willimon, *Resident Aliens* (Nashville: Abingdon, 1989), 49.

11. Ibid., 50.

12. Ibid., 51.

13. Ibid., 51.

14. Ibid., 52.

15. Thomas G. Long, *The Witness of Preaching* (Louisville: John Knox Press, 1989), 31.

16. Ibid., 33.

17. John R. W. Stott, *Between Two Worlds* (Grand Rapids: Eerdmans, 1982), 141.

18. Ibid., 145.

19. Ibid., 147.

20. Ibid., 148.

21. Ibid., 149.

22. Ibid., 149.

23. Ibid., 149.

24. Ibid., 151.

25. Eugene Lowry, *Doing Time in the Pulpit* (Nashville: Abingdon, 1985), 52.

26. Ibid., 29.

27. Ibid., 16.

28. Ibid., 88.

29. Elizabeth Achtemeier, *Preaching as Theology and Art* (Nashville: Abingdon, 1984), 62.

30. Ibid., 52.

31. Buttrick, *Homiletic*, 24.

32. Ibid., 25.

33. Ibid., 78.

34. Ibid., 140.

35. Ibid., 136.

36. Ibid., 258–62.

37. Coggan, *Preaching, the Sacrament of the Word*, 84.

38. Ibid., 75.

39. Ibid., 79.

40. Ibid., 26.

41. Ibid., 71.

42. Miller, *Spirit, Word, and Story*, 6–8.

Chapter 9: The Form of the Marketplace Sermon

1. Ralph Lewis and Gregg Lewis, *Inductive Preaching* (Westchester: Crossway Books, 1983), 122.

2. Lavonn A. Brown, "Practical Shortcuts in Sermon Preparation," from *Preaching In Today's World*, ed. James Barry (Nashville: Broadman Books, 1984), 112.

3. Lowry, *The Homiletical Plot*, 23.

4. Lowry, *Doing Time in the Pulpit*, 22.

5. Achtemeier, *Preaching as Theology and Art*, 2.

6. C. S. Lewis, *Christian Reflections* (Grand Rapids: Eerdmans, 1968), 35.

7. Ibid., 129.

8. William Blake as cited by Malcolm Muggeridge in *The Third Testament* (New York: Ballantine, 1976), 72.

9. Bruce Lockerbie, *The Cosmic Center* (Portland: Multnomah Press, 1986), 25.

10. George Santayana, *Interpretations of Poetry and Religion* (New York: HarperCollins Publishers, 1957), 6.

11. Vladimir Nabokov, *Lectures on Don Quixote* (New York: Harcourt Brace Jovanovich, 1983), 17.

12. Achtemeier, *Preaching as Theology and Art*, 51.

13. Eric Hoffer, *The Ordeal of Change* (New York: HarperCollins, 1952), 132–33.

14. Calvin Miller, "Preaching and Church Growth," in *Preaching With Confidence*, ed. James Barry (Nashville: Broadman Press, 1980), 18.

15. Howard K. Buerlein, *How To Preach More Powerful Sermons* (Philadelphia: Westminster, 1984), 63.

16. Fred Craddock, *Preaching* (Nashville: Abingdon, 1985), 64.

Afterword

1. Flannery O'Connor as quoted in *Culture in Christian Perspective* by Leland Ryken (Portland: Multnomah Press, 1986), 44.

2. Ibid.

3. Bruce Lockerbie, *The Liberating Word* (Grand Rapids: Eerdmans, 1974), 44.

4. Madeleine L'Engle, *The Irrational Season* (New York: Seabury, 1977), 27.

5. Madeleine L'Engle, *Walking on Water* (Wheaton: Harold Shaw Publishers, 1980), 43–48.

6. Lockerbie, *The Liberating Word*, 73.

7. Ibid., 73.